Thinking Strategies

for the

Successful Classroom

5–7 Year Olds

Contributors:

Rosalind Curtis

Maiya Edwards

Fay Holbert

Margaret Bishop

Brilliant Publications

Publisher's Information

Brilliant Publications
www.brilliantpublications.co.uk

Sales
BEBC (Brilliant Publications)
Albion Close, Parkstone, Poole, Dorset BH12 3LL UK
Tel: 01202 712910   Fax: 0845 1309300

Editorial
Unit 10, Sparrow Hall Farm,
Edlesborough, Dunstable, Bedfordshire LU6 2ES UK

The name Brilliant Publications and its logo are registered trademarks.

Originally published in 2004 by Blake Education Pty Ltd, Australia.
Copyright © 2004 Blake Education
This edition is for sale in the United Kingdom only.

Illustrations by Greg Anderson-Clift
Cover design by Lynda Murray
Cover illustration by Sharon Scotland

ISBN: 978-1-905780-03-7

First printed in the UK 2007.

10   9   8   7   6   5   4   3   2   1

The right of Rosalind Curtis, Maiya Edwards, Fay Holbert and Margaret Bishop to be identified as co-authors of this work has been asserted by themselves in accordance with the Copyright, Designs and Patents Act 1988.

Pages 11–19, 24–25, 27–28, 30–31, 36–37, 39–40, 42–43, 48–49, 51–52, 54–55, 60–61, 63–64, 66–67, 72–73, 75–76, 78–79, 84–90, 92–96 may be photocopied by the purchasing institution or the individual teachers for classroom use only, without consent from the publisher. No other part of this book may be reproduced in any other form or for any other purpose without the prior permission of the publisher. All enquiries should be made to the publisher at the *Editorial* address above.

Acknowledgements: Blake Education and Brilliant Publications would like to thank Professor Joseph Renzulli and Professor Howard Gardner for permission to base some of the activities in this book on their theories. Professor Gardner's theories can be found in: Gardner, H, *Intelligence Reframed* (New York, Basic Books, 1999).

Contents

Introduction	4
Management Strategies for Developing Higher-level Thinking in the Mainstream Classroom	5
Bloom's Taxonomy	**20**
Bloom's Taxonomy in Literacy	23
Bloom's Taxonomy in Maths	26
Bloom's Taxonomy in PSHE	29
Creative Thinking	**32**
Creative Thinking in Literacy	35
Creative Thinking in Maths	38
Creative Thinking in Science	41
Research Skills	**44**
Research Skills in Literacy	47
Research Skills in Maths	50
Research Skills in Humanities	53
Questioning Skills and Brainstorming	**56**
Questioning Skills and Brainstorming in Literacy	59
Questioning Skills and Brainstorming in Maths	62
Questioning Skills and Brainstorming in Science	65
Renzulli's Enrichment Triad	**68**
Renzulli's Enrichment Triad in Literacy	71
Renzulli's Enrichment Triad in Maths	74
Renzulli's Enrichment Triad in Science	77
Gardner's Multiple Intelligences	**80**
Gardner's Multiple Intelligences, Activities	83

Introduction

The teaching and management strategies in this book cater for all pupils, but provide in-built opportunities for bright pupils. Just like pupils who are struggling, bright pupils have needs that must be met before they can develop personally and academically to their full potential. Some of the consequences of not catering adequately for these pupils are frustration, disruptive or aggressive behaviour, withdrawal and underachievement.

These strategies allow all pupils to actively participate in their own learning. The worksheets and task cards are ready to use or can easily be added to your existing lesson plans.

How This Book is Structured
Management Strategies for Developing Higher-level Thinking

This section describes the key management strategies for developing higher-level thinking in your classroom. Each management strategy is given a symbol which appears on the task cards and photocopiable worksheets throughout the book. In this section you'll also find helpful generic photocopiable worksheets to support these management strategies.

Teaching Strategies
Six teaching strategies are targeted:
- Bloom's Taxonomy
- Creative Thinking
- Research Skills
- Questioning Skills and Brainstorming
- Renzulli's Enrichment Triad
- Gardner's Multiple Intelligences

Each of these strategies has its own section including:
Notes These provide an overview of the methodology of the teaching strategy and its practical application in the classroom.
Activities These include a wide range of teaching activities covering the main Learning Areas. They can be undertaken exclusively, or in conjunction with activities from the other teaching-strategy sections. They could also prompt you to develop your own activities.
Task Cards and Worksheets The activities are supported by a variety of ready-to-use worksheets and task cards. Suggested management strategies are indicated by symbols in the top right-hand corner.

Management Strategies for Developing Higher-level Thinking in the Mainstream Classroom

by **Maiya Edwards**

MANAGEMENT STRATEGIES OVERVIEW

Management Strategies for Developing Higher-level Thinking in the Mainstream Classroom

As a teacher, it is difficult to predict the skills that will be of value to pupils in the future. Teaching them high-level thinking strategies will provide them with the tools necessary to navigate through the inevitable information overload, and help them to determine what information is of use to them.

Linda Silverman, the director of the Gifted Development Center in Denver, suggests that there are several approaches that work well when dealing with bright pupils in the classroom. These approaches, listed below, work equally well with all pupils and will help to create a classroom environment that fosters higher-order thinking skills.

Find out what they know before you teach them

This will prevent reteaching what a pupil already knows.

Remove drill from their lives

Bright pupils learn and retain a concept the first time it is presented to them. Allow them to move on to something else while you consolidate concepts with the rest of the class.

Pace instruction at the rate of the learner

Pupils learn at different rates. Allow them to progress at their own rate.

Use discovery learning techniques

Use Inductive Learning strategies (such as those explained in the Bloom's Taxonomy model) to allow pupils to use thinking skills to reach conclusions.

Allow them to arrive at answers in their own way

Bright pupils enjoy devising their own problem-solving techniques.

Allow pupils to form their own cooperative learning groups

Avoid always making the brightest pupil in the group responsible for the whole group's learning. Allow them to sometimes choose their own groups and work with other bright, motivated pupils.

Design an individual education plan

This will cater for different learning rates.

Teach them the art of argument

Since bright pupils have a tendency to argue anyway, teach them to understand when it is appropriate to argue and also to understand the reaction of others to their argumentativeness.

Allow pupils to observe

Provide pupils with opportunities to observe and don't demand immediate answers.

Be flexible in designing programmes

Provide your pupils with a variety of programme alternatives, such as independent study, special classes, mentoring and enrichment and extension activities.

As many bright pupils are unable to achieve their full potential in the regular classroom, they can often become frustrated and begin to exhibit disruptive or aggressive behaviour. Others withdraw from class activities, or deliberately mask their ability.

Providing activities for the entire class does not mean that the activities need to limit bright pupils to make them conform. These classroom-management strategies have been devised to allow for implementation of all of the key educational qualities referred to above. The strategies are practical, flexible and easy to implement.

Each strategy has been given an easily recognizable symbol (see the next four pages) so that when these strategies are applied to the 'task card' and 'worksheet' activities in this book, you will know immediately how to organize your classroom.

Management Strategies for Developing Higher-level Thinking in the Mainstream Classroom

A range of classroom-management strategies could be employed to promote and encourage the development of the talent of the pupils in your class. Any of the strategies listed below would help to achieve a positive classroom environment.

Management Strategies Suitable for the Mainstream Classroom

▼ Enrichment and Extension Activities

→ Learning/Interest Centres

● Contracts

❖ Independent Research

■ Parent Involvement

✖ Peer Tutoring

★ Competitions and Awards

◗ Mentoring

✴ Team Teaching

◆ Withdrawal from classroom

⊃ Mixed-ability Grouping

✚ Same-ability Grouping

▲ Vertical Grouping

♣ Field Trips

Below is a sample page from the sections that follow. The symbols relating to the classroom strategies are at the top of each worksheet or task card.

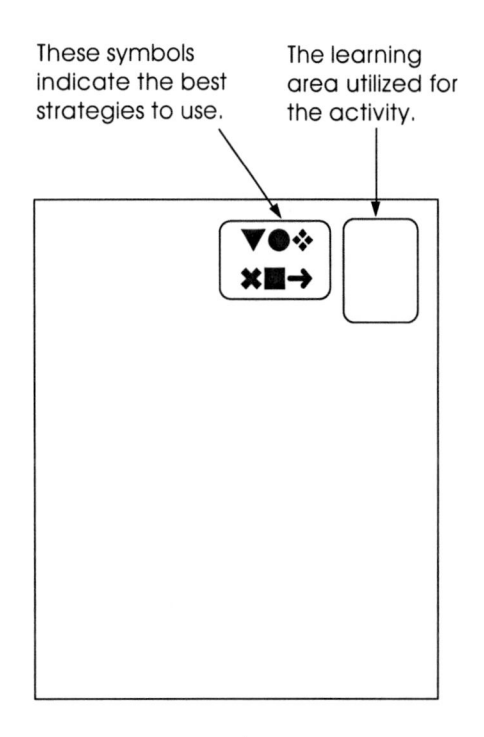

These symbols indicate the best strategies to use.

The learning area utilized for the activity.

Other broader strategies, less suitable for the classroom are listed below.

Management Strategies Suitable for the Whole-School Approach

♦ Liaison with feeder secondary school
♦ Out-of-school same-ability groups
♦ In-school same-ability groups
♦ Camps
♦ Specialist classes
♦ Extra-curriculum activities
♦ Competitions and awards

Class Programming

♦ Curriculum compacting
♦ Acceleration

Brilliant Publications Thinking Strategies for the Successful Classroom, 5–7 Year Olds

Management Strategies for Developing Higher-level Thinking in the Mainstream Classroom

1 ▼ Enrichment and Extension Activities

These can be provided in all subject areas in a variety of ways:

- Task cards or worksheets for higher-level thinking skills
- Research tasks
- Special 'challenge' days
- Independent projects
- Parent or mentor involvement

2 → Learning/Interest Centres

These can be established in a corner of the classroom, and designed to generate interest in a particular topic. They can:

- Concentrate on one specific aspect of work being studied, such as 'Weather Patterns'
- Accommodate a special interest, such as 'Dinosaurs'
- Extend certain skills, such as Advanced Language/Mathematical Skills or Thinking Skills

See worksheets 4, 5, 6

3 ● Contracts

Pupils can be given a range of activities to complete which are set out around the room. Each pupil is given a list of the activities and asked to mark off each one as it is completed. The flexibility of this contract system appeals to the more capable pupil.

Contracts also have the advantage of being either teacher initiated or pupil initiated. The teacher can set defined, targeted tasks or can allow the pupils to pursue their own interests with some guidance. There is also flexibility in the time allowed for the contract. A contract can be extended over many weeks or set as a one night task.

See worksheets 1, 2, 3, 4, 7

4 ❖ Independent Research

Independent research provides an opportunity either within the school day or over a longer period to develop personal competencies through individual experiences. It may also involve interaction with others when appropriate. The research topic can be teacher initiated or pupil initiated.

It allows the pupil to launch an in-depth investigation into something that they want to find out more about without constant supervision. It also encourages the pupil to use self-initiative and to employ their own style of learning to produce results.

The teacher's role changes from being the source of all knowledge to that of a facilitator and consultant.

See worksheets 1, 2, 3, 4, 7

5 ■ Parent Involvement

Establishing and maintaining a register of parents' interests, abilities and availability can be invaluable when planning a work-activities scheme for the brighter pupils in the classroom. Parents can be used to supervise same-ability groups or extension activities and to encourage the exploration of individual interest areas. Some of the ways that parents could be kept abreast of classroom activities are newsletters, resource packs and information evenings.

See worksheet 9

Management Strategies for Developing Higher-level Thinking in the Mainstream Classroom

6 ✖ Peer Tutoring

The more capable pupils can be paired with underachievers for some activities. This can be mutually beneficial for both pupils. The brighter pupils must develop an ability to clearly communicate an understanding of a topic or problem, while the underachiever receives the benefit of one-to-one coaching.

Outside the mainstream classroom, you can pair more able, older pupils with bright younger pupils. For example, pairing Year 6 pupils with Year 1 pupils works particularly well. The pupils could be paired for 30 to 60 minutes per week for activities such as writing, ICT, art or thinking games.

7 ★ Competitions and Awards

Competition and Award schemes such as 'Young Innovator of the Year' and 'Tournament of the Minds' offer enrichment opportunities for all pupils, but particularly the brighter pupils. Pupils within the mainstream classroom could be provided with activities to prepare them for these tournaments and competitions.

Intra-class competitions and awards are a dynamic means of extending the entire class. There is a wide range of options, some of which are:

- 30-minute quiz challenges
- Knock-out quiz challenges throughout the term or year.
- Award schemes for independent research tasks. (Bronze award for a written and pictorial presentation; Silver if something extra is included, such as a model; and Gold if the project is outstanding.)
- Individual point scoring for tasks throughout the year. This scheme works well for all pupils in the mainstream classroom as points can be awarded for both outstanding work, additional work, improvement, effort, positive attitudes, or helping others. Points can be exchanged for play money at the end of each term, and pupils can bid at a class auction for donated items such as books, tickets or toys; or 'buy' privileges, such as extra computer time.

8 ◗ Mentoring

These schemes link individual pupils with community members who have expertise in certain areas. Teachers can establish their own database of suitable people or seek the assistance of their Regional Partnership of the National Academy for Gifted and Talented Youth. Mentors can also talk to the class on given interest areas and participate in some follow-up activities. This is a very productive way of inspiring excellence and encouraging independent interests.

9 ✲ Team Teaching

Pupils with various interests and talents meet with different teachers who specialize in specific subject areas. An excellent way to implement this is for three teachers to nominate three different fields of interest. The pupils then select which area of interest to pursue. This can be scheduled into the standard teaching week and run for two or three lessons, with a suitable assessment regime at its conclusion.

10 ◆ Withdrawal from Classroom

Very exceptional pupils (or 'gifted' pupils) can be withdrawn from a mixed-ability class for instruction with other more advanced pupils. This instruction can be provided by a specially appointed teacher or tutor, or a volunteer.

Management Strategies for Developing Higher-level Thinking in the Mainstream Classroom

11 ⊃ Mixed-ability Grouping

When working on class assignments, the pupils are placed in groups with a range of abilities. The more able pupils assume the leadership roles, with the others given the tasks of writing and reporting. Roles can also be interchangeable, or they can be rotated so that an even amount of work is done in all aspects of a task. An ideal number for mixed-ability groupings is three to five.

See worksheet 4

12 ✚ Same-ability Grouping

All pupils can be grouped according to their relative ability in the classroom. Higher-ability pupils can occasionally be grouped for full-time instruction within a mixed-ability classroom. This works well when compacting a curriculum for the brighter pupils so that they are able to progress at their own rate.

13 ▲ Vertical Grouping

In classrooms that already contain several year groups, bright pupils of different ages can be combined with others who have similar interests, abilities and aptitudes.

See worksheet 4

14 ♣ Field Trips

This involves off-campus excursions to meet with experts in various fields, for example museum experts, marine biologists or geologists. Field trips can provide an excellent basis for both same-ability groups projects or independent research projects.

Self-evaluation

It should be remembered that self-evaluation is a very powerful form of assessment and should be an essential component of every classroom evaluation process.

This has been incorporated into the worksheets on the following pages.

Worksheets

A range of worksheets has been provided which can be used to assess and encourage pupils when using the above management strategies.

They are not activities in themselves but are designed to support the various teaching strategies presented in the book.

Teacher Records

For your own records and so that you can show parents that you have given their children the opportunity to express the full range of skills, we have provided an individual record sheet suitable for each pupil as well as a class record sheet.

See worksheets 7 and 8

Name: _____

My Research Contract

Research Title: _____

Starting Date: _____ Completion Date: _____

Subject Area: _____

Brief Description: _____

Resources to be used: _____

Method of final presentation: _____

School time allocated to independent research: _____

Home time allocated to independent research: _____

Pupil's Signature: _____

Teacher's Signature: _____

Self-evaluation

The best thing about my independent research was: _____
_____
_____

The thing I found hardest to do was: _____
_____
_____

I could improve this by: _____
_____
_____

Teacher Comment

MANAGEMENT STRATEGIES
Worksheet 1

This page may be photocopied for use by the purchasing institution only.
© Blake Education Pty Ltd. 2004

Brilliant Publications — Thinking Strategies for the Successful Classroom, 5–7 Year Olds — 11

MANAGEMENT STRATEGIES — Worksheet 2

Name: _____

My Contract

My contract is to _____

I will start on _____ and finish by _____

✓ When finished	What I will do	How I feel about my work

Teacher Comment

Name:

MANAGEMENT STRATEGIES Worksheet 3

My Research Checklist

Tick (✓) the methods you have used for your independent research and hand this sheet in with your final presentation.

- ☐ Brainstorming
- ☐ Concept Mapping
- ☐ Library Research
- ☐ Interviewing
- ☐ Survey
- ☐ Questionnaire
- ☐ Experiment
- ☐ Graphs/Tables

Your final methods of presentation can be very simple or quite complex. Here are some suggestions. Circle the methods you will use.

- Written Report
- Videotape
- Scrapbook
- Letter
- Musical Composition
- Model
- Demonstration
- Advertisement
- Play/TV Show
- Comic Strip
- Magazine
- Invention
- Panel Discussion

- ☐ Final Method of Presentation Chosen
- ☐ Final Presentation
- ☐ Own Evaluation of the Independent Study
- ☐ Teacher Evaluation of the Independent Study

Brilliant Publications — Thinking Strategies for the Successful Classroom, 5–7 Year Olds

MANAGEMENT STRATEGIES Worksheet 4

Self-evaluation

Name: _____

Checklist for Group Work

Other Group Members: _____

☐ I contributed new ideas. The best idea was _____

☐ I listened to the ideas of others. The best idea was _____

☐ I encouraged others in my group. This was by _____

☐ Something I could improve on is _____

_____

_____

Name: _____

Questionnaire for Learning/Interest Centres or Enrichment Activities

Task: _____ Time taken: _____

How I did the activity and what I thought of it: _____

_____

_____

Future activities I would like included: _____

_____

_____

14   Thinking Strategies for the Successful Classroom, 5–7 Year Olds   Brilliant Publications

This page may be photocopied for use by the purchasing institution only.
© Blake Education Pty Ltd. 2004

Name:

Learning/Interest Centre Evaluation Sheet

MANAGEMENT STRATEGIES
Worksheet 5

ACTIVITY	DATE COMPLETED	EVALUATION (for example: too hard, too easy, boring, interesting)

Teacher Comment

This page may be photocopied for use by the purchasing institution only.
© Blake Education Pty Ltd. 2004

Brilliant Publications Thinking Strategies for the Successful Classroom, 5–7 Year Olds

MANAGEMENT STRATEGIES
Worksheet 6

Name:

Concept Mapping

| IDEA | IDEA | IDEA | IDEA |

SUB-TOPIC _____

SUB-TOPIC _____

TOPIC _____

SUB-TOPIC _____

SUB-TOPIC _____

| IDEA | IDEA | IDEA | IDEA |

16   Thinking Strategies for the Successful Classroom, 5–7 Year Olds   Brilliant Publications

Individual Record Sheet

Extension Procedures

MANAGEMENT STRATEGIES Worksheet 7

Pupil's Name: _____ Year: _____

Pupils should complete one task card or worksheet from each extension procedure.

THINKING STRATEGY	TASK CARDS/WORKSHEETS COMPLETED (Indicate below the worksheet/task card completed)
Bloom's Taxonomy (BT)	
Creative Thinking (CT)	
Research Skills (R)	
Questioning/Brainstorming (QB)	
Renzulli's Enrichment Triad (RT)	
Gardner's Multiple Intelligences (GI)	

Teacher Comment

MANAGEMENT STRATEGIES — Worksheet 8

Class Record Sheet
Extension Procedures

Check that each pupil has completed at least one task card or worksheet from each extension procedure.

PUPIL'S NAME	BT	CT	R	QB	RT	GI	COMMENT

Register of Parents' Interests

PARENT'S NAME	CHILD	CONTACT DETAILS	AVAILABILITY	AREA/S OF INTEREST

Bloom's Taxonomy

by **Maiya Edwards**

Overview for the Classroom Teacher

BLOOM'S TAXONOMY NOTES

Bloom's Taxonomy

This model is one of the most frequently used extension procedures for the development of higher-level thinking skills. These skills are applicable to any subject, and to any level of education, from pre-school to higher education. Many varied teaching and learning activities can be developed using this as the basis.

The model enables *all* pupils to work through the process of developing a concept, with the more advanced pupils spending longer at the higher levels than the average student.

The thought processes involved in the different levels are:

1. KNOWLEDGE – recognize, list, name, read, absorb.
2. COMPREHENSION – restate, describe, identify, review, explain.
3. APPLICATION – apply, illustrate, connect, develop, use.
4. ANALYSIS – interpret, categorize, contrast, compare, classify.
5. SYNTHESIS – plan, create, invent, modify, revise.
6. EVALUATION – judge, recommend, assess, criticize, justify.

Average Pupil

1. Knowing and recalling specific facts.
2. Understanding the meaning from given information.
3. Using previously learned information in new situations.

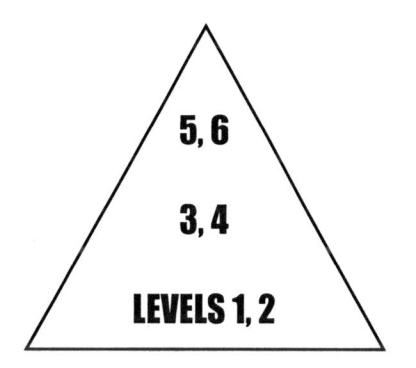

(Triangle: 5, 6 / 3, 4 / LEVELS 1, 2)

Talented Pupil

4. Breaking up the whole into parts.
5. Putting together the parts to form a new whole.
6. Making value judgements.

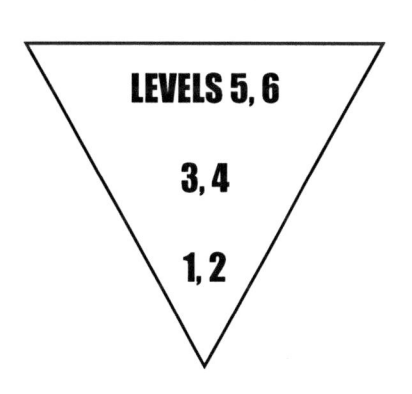

(Inverted triangle: LEVELS 5, 6 / 3, 4 / 1, 2)

Brilliant Publications — Thinking Strategies for the Successful Classroom, 5–7 Year Olds

BLOOM'S TAXONOMY NOTES

Overview for the Classroom Teacher

From Convergent to Divergent Thinking

Use the actions . . . . to achieve these outcomes.

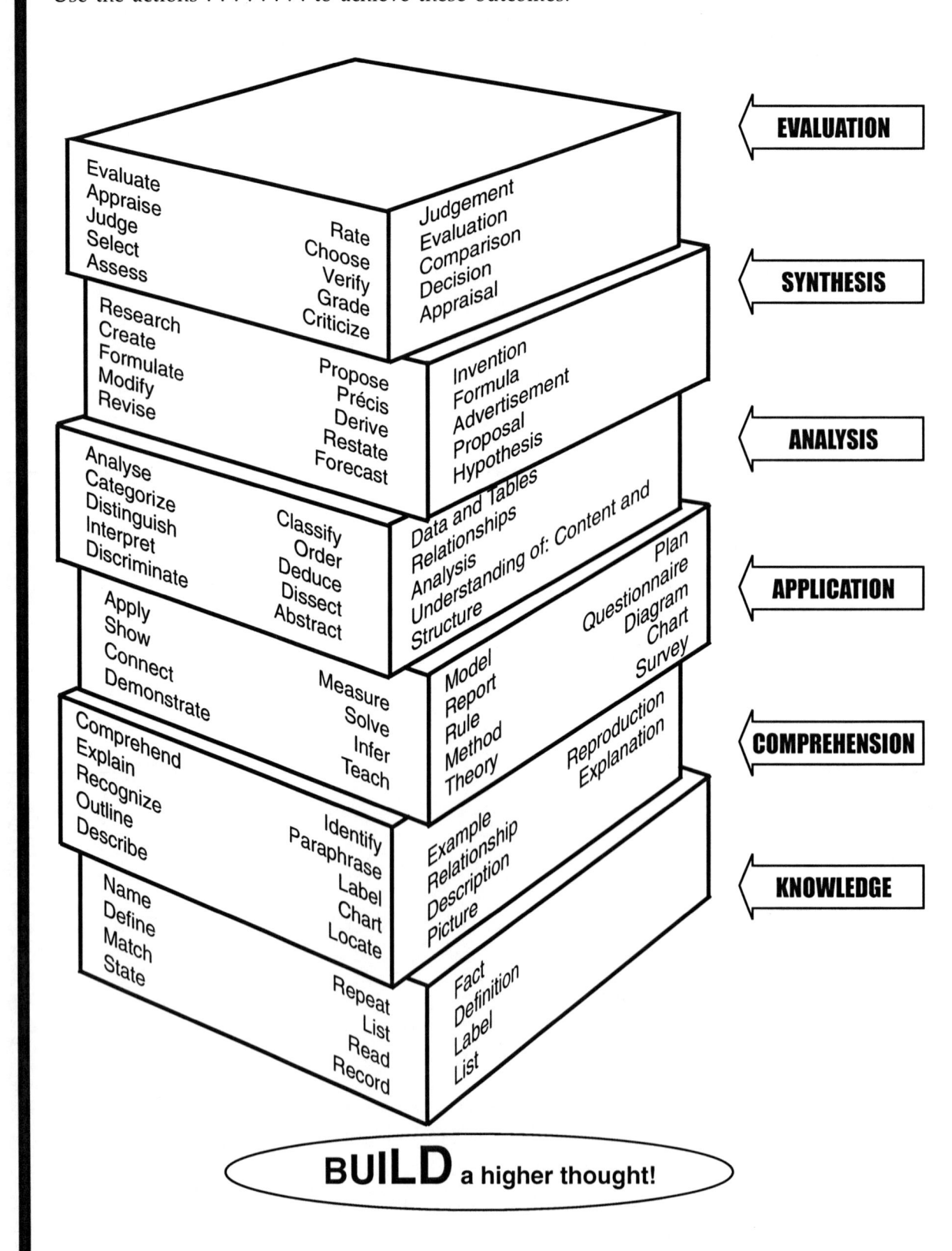

EVALUATION
- Evaluate, Appraise, Judge, Select, Assess
- Rate, Choose, Verify, Grade, Criticize
- Judgement, Evaluation, Comparison, Decision, Appraisal

SYNTHESIS
- Research, Create, Formulate, Modify, Revise
- Propose, Précis, Derive, Restate, Forecast
- Invention, Formula, Advertisement, Proposal, Hypothesis

ANALYSIS
- Analyse, Categorize, Distinguish, Interpret, Discriminate
- Classify, Order, Deduce, Dissect, Abstract
- Data and Tables, Relationships, Analysis, Understanding of: Content and Structure

APPLICATION
- Apply, Show, Connect, Demonstrate
- Measure, Solve, Infer, Teach
- Model, Report, Rule, Method, Theory
- Plan, Questionnaire, Diagram, Chart, Survey

COMPREHENSION
- Comprehend, Explain, Recognize, Outline, Describe
- Identify, Paraphrase, Label, Chart, Locate
- Example, Relationship, Description, Picture
- Reproduction, Explanation

KNOWLEDGE
- Name, Define, Match, State
- Repeat, List, Read, Record
- Fact, Definition, Label, List

BUILD a higher thought!

Thinking Strategies for the Successful Classroom, 5–7 Year Olds — Brilliant Publications

Bloom's Taxonomy in Literacy

Theme: Travel

Knowledge

- Ask pupils to list all the different ways people can travel.
- Ask children to label different forms of transport.
- Ask pupils to brainstorm different types of cars.

Comprehension

- Ask pupils to identify different forms of transport from photographs. These can be placed around the room.
- Pupils can describe their family car.
- Encourage pupils to retell some facts they know about different forms of transport.

Application

- Ask pupils to locate their nearest train station.
- Ask them to show the class the route they travel to school.
- Design a class mural showing all the different forms of transport.

Analysis

- Ask children to categorize the different forms of travel under the headings of AIR, SEA, RAIL, ROAD.
- Pupils can compare old forms of travel with modern forms.
- Make a class chart showing how pupils travel to school.

Synthesis

- Ask the class to predict how pupils will travel to school in the future.
- Challenge pupils to think of what would happen if there were no more cars in the world.
- Ask children to mime a different way to travel.

Evaluation

- Pupils can create little books showing their favourite ways to travel, for example by train, car or on horseback.
- Ask pupils to calculate how long it takes them to get to school. Are there ways they could reduce this time?
- Ask pupils to choose the best way to travel from their home to the Millennium Stadium (in Cardiff) or a major sports venue in their town or city.

BLOOM'S TAXONOMY — Literacy — Worksheet 10

Name:

Management Strategies:

Travel

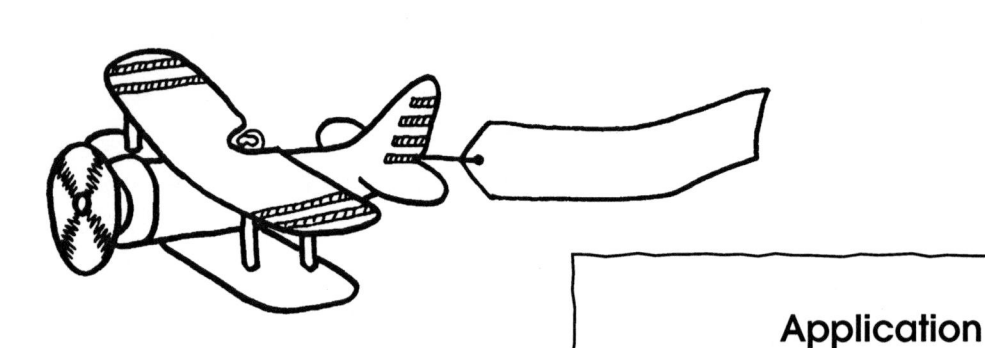

Knowledge
How many ways can you travel from one place to another?

List all the ways you know.

_____
_____
_____
_____
_____
_____
_____
_____
_____
_____
_____
_____
_____

Application
Make a model of your family car.

Comprehension
Explain the main method you use to get home from school.

_____
_____
_____
_____
_____
_____
_____
_____
_____
_____

Thinking Strategies for the Successful Classroom, 5–7 Year Olds

Name:

Management Strategies:

BLOOM'S TAXONOMY
Literacy
Worksheet 11

Travel

Synthesis

Invent a new way you could come to school.

Analysis

Survey the class to find out how many different ways they travel to school.

Number   Method
_____   _____
_____   _____
_____   _____
_____   _____
_____   _____
_____   _____
_____   _____

Evaluation

What changes would you recommend to road rules to prevent traffic accidents?

_____
_____
_____
_____
_____
_____
_____
_____
_____
_____
_____
_____
_____
_____
_____
_____
_____
_____

Brilliant Publications   Thinking Strategies for the Successful Classroom, 5–7 Year Olds

Bloom's Taxonomy in Maths

Knowledge

♦ Use Number Rhymes and Finger Plays to teach concepts of counting and number facts.

Examples:

> **Number**
> Ten little fingers
> Ten little toes
> Two little eyes and
> One little nose.
> One little mouth and
> Why I declare!
> Here are two little ears
> Hiding under my hair.

> **Subtraction**
> Ten ships sailing,
> sailing on the sea.
> One sailed far away
> and waved goodbye to me.

> **Time**
> My face is big
> I tick all day
> When my hands go round
> What do I say?

Comprehension

♦ Ask pupils to find objects in the classroom to divide into the following categories: big and little, rough and smooth, square and round.

♦ Ask pupils to give examples of ways they could count to 20. Suggest by ones, then see if pupils can think of counting by twos, fives, tens and so on.

Application

♦ Draw a picture (such as the sun, a bell, or a box) on the board and ask pupils to colour exactly half the picture.

♦ Ask one pupil to teach another how to work out: 10 – 4. Encourage them to use concrete objects to demonstrate. For example: put out 10 pencils and take away four to show that there are six left.

Analysis

♦ Challenge pupils to find the relationship between 11 and 33.

♦ Ask them to classify all the objects in the learning centre according to weight.

Synthesis

♦ 6 x 2 = 12. Challenge pupils to think of different formulae for arriving at the number 12.

♦ Ask pupils to plan a finger-puppet show to teach some number facts. Make a few suggestions about how they could decorate their fingers to represent different characters. Discuss ideas about which facts could be taught. They could use existing rhymes (such as the ones mentioned under 'Knowledge') as a basis for making up their own.

♦ Ask pupils to find a new way to measure the width of the classroom.

Evaluation

♦ Ask pupils to recommend the best way to work out how many different pets each pupil in the class has. For example they could ask each child individually and add these up, ask the class to raise their hands, or set out a simple questionnaire for each pupil to fill in.

Bloom's Taxonomy in Maths

Comprehension, Application, Analysis

Space

Draw the shadow of the tree.

Money

Cover each coin with the real one.

Circle the one that is worth the most.
What do you notice about it?

Patterns

Complete the patterns.

Brilliant Publications — Thinking Strategies for the Successful Classroom, 5–7 Year Olds

Bloom's Taxonomy in Maths

Analysis, Synthesis, Evaluation

Measurement

Write the days of the week in the correct order.

_____

_____

_____

Circle the day you like the most. Circle the day you like the least.

Number

Cross out three balloons.

Cross out five flowers.

8 take away 3 leaves ____ .

9 take away 5 leaves ____ .

Time

What takes the longest time to do?

Put these in the correct order (1 longest – 3 shortest):

☐ Brush your teeth ☐ Blink your eye ☐ Walk to school

Bloom's Taxonomy in PSHE

Theme: Things We Do Every Day

Knowledge

- Ask pupils to tell you some of the things they do every day. Encourage ideas by suggesting: we eat, we wash, we sleep.

Comprehension

- Have pupils cut out pictures from magazines which represent things they do every day.
- Ask them to draw pictures of things they do every day.
- Have them mime actions of what they do every day. Challenge the class to identify the action.

Application

- Talk about things pupils do every day at school, such as reading. Ask them what they read and how they read.
- Suggest that pupils make a little book about themselves for the other pupils to read. Call it 'My Favourite Things to Do Every Day'.

Analysis

- Read *How Do I Put It On* by Shigeo Wantanabe and Yasuo Ohtomo (published by Puffin Books). This is a picture book about getting dressed.
- Ask pupils, 'What does the bear put on first?'
- 'What does the bear put on his ear?'
- 'How do you get dressed?'
- If this book is not available, ask pupils to analyse their own process of getting dressed each morning.

Synthesis

- Ask pupils to create their own books about what they eat every day by cutting photographs from a magazine and sticking these into a book. They can write their own captions underneath, such as 'I eat cereal for breakfast'.
- Provide old socks, buttons and wool for pupils to make sock puppets. In groups of four to five they can then make up a puppet show about a family eating breakfast. Suggest that some groups have their puppet family eating an unhealthy breakfast, while others are eating a healthy breakfast. (Link with the 'Evaluation' activity below.)

Evaluation

- Ask pupils which foods are healthy to eat and which are unhealthy. List them on the board and discuss reasons for their choices.
- Ask them to think about their own diets and decide whether they are eating food that is good for them.

BLOOM'S TAXONOMY
PSHE
Worksheet 12

Name: _____

Management Strategies:
▼ → ● ■
✖ ✦ ↩ ▲

Getting Dressed

TASK: Write in each step as you get dressed.

Then draw a picture of yourself fully dressed.

1 First I _____

2 Next I _____

3 Then I _____

4 Then I _____

5 Finally I _____

Now I am dressed!

Name:

Management Strategies:
▼ →
● ↩

BLOOM'S TAXONOMY
PSHE
Worksheet 13

Eating

Warm-up Task: Which of these foods would you like to eat for lunch?
Answer **Yes** or **No**

1　A cheese sandwich　_____
2　A bucket of nails　_____
3　Leaves　_____
4　An apple　_____
5　Yoghurt　_____
6　Snail sausages　_____
7　Grapes　_____
8　A chocolate worm　_____
9　A banana　_____
10　Spider jelly　_____

What to Do: Imagine you can eat anything you want for breakfast.
List below and then draw a picture of each one.

I would eat:

1 _____　2 _____　3 _____

Brilliant Publications　Thinking Strategies for the Successful Classroom, 5–7 Year Olds

Creative Thinking

by Maiya Edwards

Overview for the Classroom Teacher

CREATIVE THINKING NOTES

Creative Thinking Skills

In this section, we try to move away from verbal and deductive skills and convergent thinking at factual levels to encourage originality, inductive and inferential skills and divergent thinking.

By recognizing and encouraging the potential of creative thinking in the classroom, the teacher can equip pupils with the open-ended, divergent thinking skills that are so useful in an ever-changing world.

Creativity can be developed in all pupils. This can be done by encouraging pupils to become independent thinkers who can modify, adapt and improve the classroom environment. Teachers should encourage adventure and speculation by creating a positive atmosphere in which there is freedom to reflect, experiment and take risks.

We can look at the creative process in five stages. Each of these stages involves the thinking skills and feelings which make up creativity.

Problem Awareness

This stage requires the ability to recognize that a problem exists, as well as **sensitivity** and **awareness**.

Problem Definition

The second stage involves stating a problem in a meaningful way so that it is easily understood and therefore requires **imagination**, **curiosity** and **originality**.

Incubation of Ideas

The third stage involves the production of intuitive and original possible answers before the facts have been checked out. Therefore, this synthesizing process of blending the old with the new requires **fluency, flexibility, originality, elaboration, risk-taking** and **imagination**.

Illumination

The fourth stage requires the **awareness** necessary to provide an instant insight into the solution, often referred to as the 'Aha!' moment.

Evaluation

The final stage requires the **perseverance** to evaluate the validity and full impact of the ideas generated.

Encouragement of creativity requires activities to challenge both 'thinking skills' and 'emotional responses'. This can be done by providing a supportive and stimulating classroom environment which will nurture these processes. On the following page are some ways in which the creative elements of thinking and emotional response can be enhanced.

Creativity Catalysts can be used to generate innovative and original ideas.

CREATIVE THINKING NOTES

Overview for the Classroom Teacher

Creativity Catalysts

Fluency

This initial stage combines the thinking skill of fluency with the emotional responses of imagination, curiosity and originality to generate many different ideas, possibilities and solutions.

Creativity Catalysts:

- How many ways ... ?
- List all the possible uses ...
- Think of all the problems ...
- Give as many ideas as you can ...
- Add to this list ...

Flexibility

This stage combines the thinking skill of flexibility with the emotional response of sensitivity to allow the pupil to blend the old with the new, and to see things from many different points of view.

Creativity Catalysts:

- What is the relationship between... ?
- What would it be like if you were ... ?
- Categorize ...
- Rearrange ...
- Substitute ...

Originality

This stage combines the thinking skill of originality with the emotional responses of risk-taking and imagination. It encourages pupils to be inventive and use unique and unexpected approaches.

Creativity Catalysts:

- Create ...
- Design a different way to ...
- How would you ... ?
- Invent ...
- Predict ...

Elaboration

This final stage combines the thinking skill of elaboration with the emotional responses of awareness and perseverance. It encourages pupils to expand, develop and add to ideas and materials.

Creativity Catalysts:

- Add details to ...
- Plan ...
- Expand ...
- Combine ...
- Decide ...

For more useful classroom catalysts, use the mnemonic **CREATIVITY** to generate further extension activities.

C Combine: integrate, merge, fuse, brew, synthesize, amalgamate

R Reverse: transpose, invert, transfer, exchange, return, contradict

E Enlarge: magnify, expand, multiply, exaggerate, spread, repeat

A Adapt: suit, conform, modify, alter, emulate, copy, reconcile

T Tinier: minimize, streamline, shrink, squeeze, eliminate, understate

I Instead of: substitute, swap, replace, exchange, alternate, supplant

V Viewpoint change: other eyes, other directions, more optimistically, more pessimistically

I In another sequence: rotate, rearrange, bypass, vary, submerge, reschedule

T To other uses: change, modify, rework, other values and locations

Y Yes!: affirm, agree, endorse, concur, approve, consent, ratify, corroborate

Creative Thinking in Literacy

Theme: Circus

Fluency

- Ask 'How many circus words can you think of in two minutes?'
- Find out how many pupils in the class have been to the circus.
- Ask them to list the types of acts they saw.
- Have pupils list all the people associated with the circus. Remind them that there are many behind-the-scenes people, such as those who look after the animals, those who make the costumes and those who sell food and tickets.
- Ask pupils to list five books about the circus.

Flexibility

- Ask pupils to separate the list of circus people into different categories, such as funny acts, dangerous acts and so on.
- Have pupils describe what a juggler does.
- Ask 'What sort of things would an acrobat need to know?'
- Pupils can write a story about 'My First Circus' from the point of view of a clown who is performing in one of the acts.

Originality

- Ask pupils to describe the act that a fire-eating trapeze artist would perform. Ask them for other funny combinations.
- Ask them to list all the ways to make: a) a clown laugh; b) a crowd cheer.
- Pupils can combine the attributes of an umbrella, a shopping trolley and a banana to create a brand-new circus act.
- Ask pupils to describe what a circus will look like 100 years from now.
- Pupils can design a flag for a circus.
- Ask pupils to invent a story about a heroic act by a tightrope-walker.

Elaboration

- Ask pupils to list 10 different uses for a circus tent.
- Pupils can write out a job application for a clown.
- Ask 'If you could join a circus, what is the thing you would most like to do? Why is this your favourite?'
- Put pupils in pairs and ask them to create a way to make the game of *Snakes and Ladders* into an exciting circus act.
- Give pupils the following beginning to a story and ask them to complete it: 'It was my first visit to the circus. I was very excited. Suddenly the crowd went quiet. I looked up and could not believe my eyes … .'

Creative Thinking in Literacy

The Circus

It is good to have animal acts in a circus. What do you think? List five good things and five bad things about having animals in a circus.

Clowns

How could a clown use these to be funny?

An old shoe

A box

A loaf of bread

Elephants

Make up five questions for this answer:

An elephant.

What do you think?

What do a juggler and a computer have in common?

Creative Thinking in Literacy

CREATIVE THINKING — Literacy **TASK CARDS**

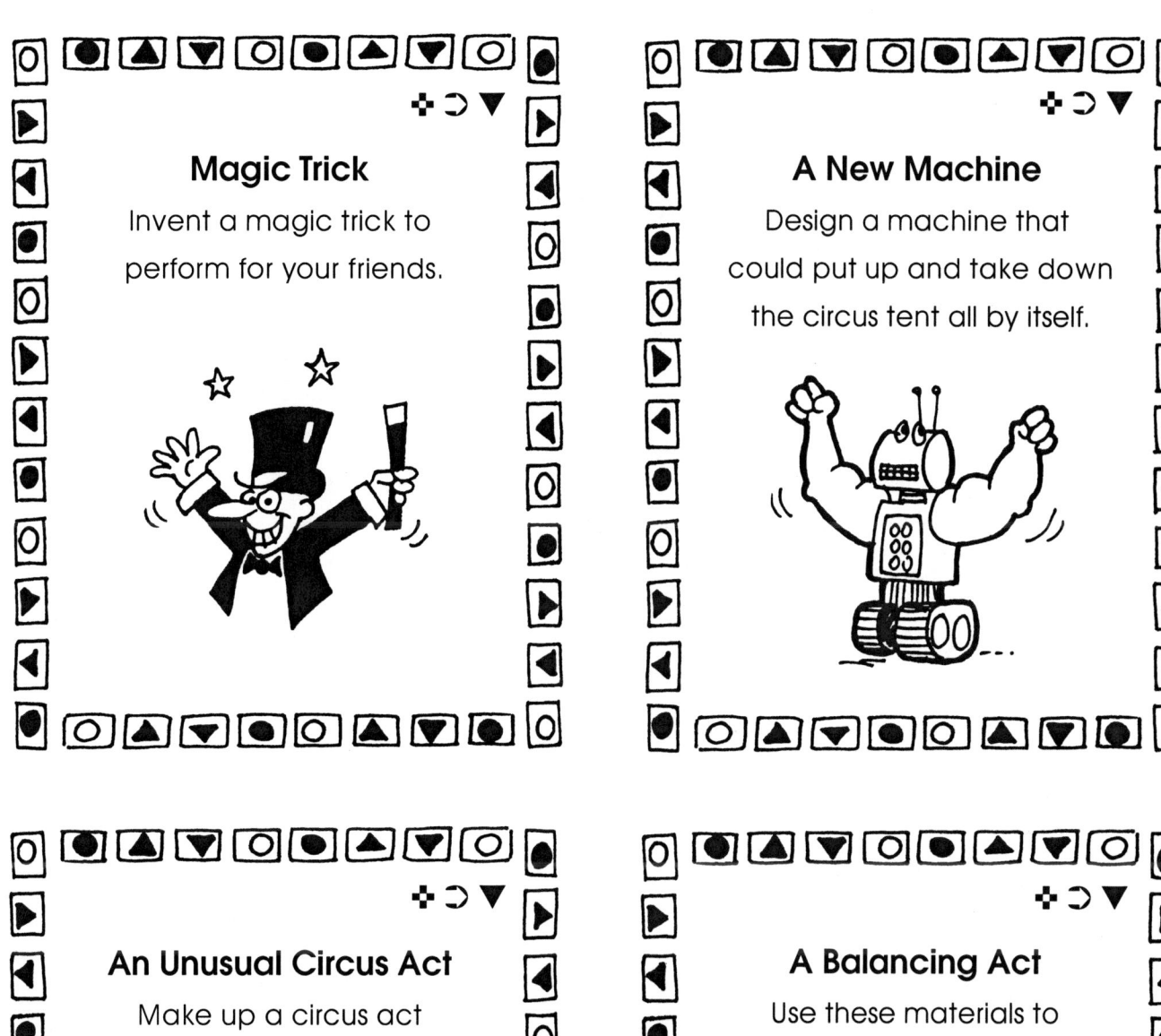

Magic Trick
Invent a magic trick to perform for your friends.

A New Machine
Design a machine that could put up and take down the circus tent all by itself.

An Unusual Circus Act
Make up a circus act that could be performed by Jack, the Beanstalk and the Giant.

A Balancing Act
Use these materials to construct something that a tightrope-walker could use in their circus act:
A newspaper
A wheelbarrow
2 balloons

CREATIVE THINKING — **Maths** — **ACTIVITIES**

Creative Thinking in Maths

Encourage creative thinking in maths by beginning each lesson with a quick challenge to pupils related to the unit of work they are about to study. This will focus pupils' thinking and encourage active participation in the lesson right from the start. It will also help to create a more positive attitude towards the learning process.

Fluency

Encourage pupils to think about the thinking skills and inquiry processes required for solving problems. Encourage them to brainstorm ideas and come up with a lot of solutions and possibilities. Stimulate discussion with questions like:

♦ How many round things can you list in two minutes?

♦ List all the possible uses for a ruler.

♦ Can you name all the objects with angles in the classroom?

♦ List all the objects in the classroom that are different solid shapes. For example a pencil is cylindrical.

Flexibility

Expand brainstorming activities by adapting and extending them. Suggestions:

♦ Group the words brainstormed about shapes into as many different categories as you can. For example: big and little, smooth and rough, solid and hollow.

♦ Have pupils think of some new uses for a 50-pence piece.

♦ Compare a cube to a sphere. How are they the same? How are they different?

♦ Ask pupils to think of reasons why coins are round. Ask them to suggest other shapes they could be. Discuss the problems and benefits.

Originality

Encourage originality by asking open-ended questions, providing pupils with more opportunities to think in the abstract and rewarding creative and innovative solutions. Suggest to the pupils:

♦ Pair up and then design a maths puzzle for your partner to solve.

♦ Invent new names for the days of the week.

♦ Imagine you are only 30 centimetres tall. How would the world be different?

♦ Design a new shape for a milk bottle.

♦ What would our houses look like if they had no corners?

Elaboration

Encourage pupils to work in groups or individually to reflect upon the previous three processes. Ask them to look at alternatives, expand on ideas and add more details with activities such as those suggested below:

♦ Draw a triangle. Add details to make it into a soft toy.

♦ Add to the number 5 to make it into an interesting pattern.

♦ You have won £50. You have to spend it all on your dog. Describe how you would spend your money.

♦ Imagine what would happen if you changed the shape of the bat used in rounders to a box shape and the ball to a pyramid shape. Describe how the game would change.

Creative Thinking in Maths

CREATIVE THINKING Maths TASK CARDS

Space

Make a train like the one shown using cylinders of different sizes.

How many cylinders make your train?

Measurement

Name something that takes longer than:

Eating an ice cream _____

Making your bed _____

Brushing your teeth _____

Time

Name the three months of summer.

_____

_____

_____

Draw a summer picture.

Shapes

The four shapes shown below are:

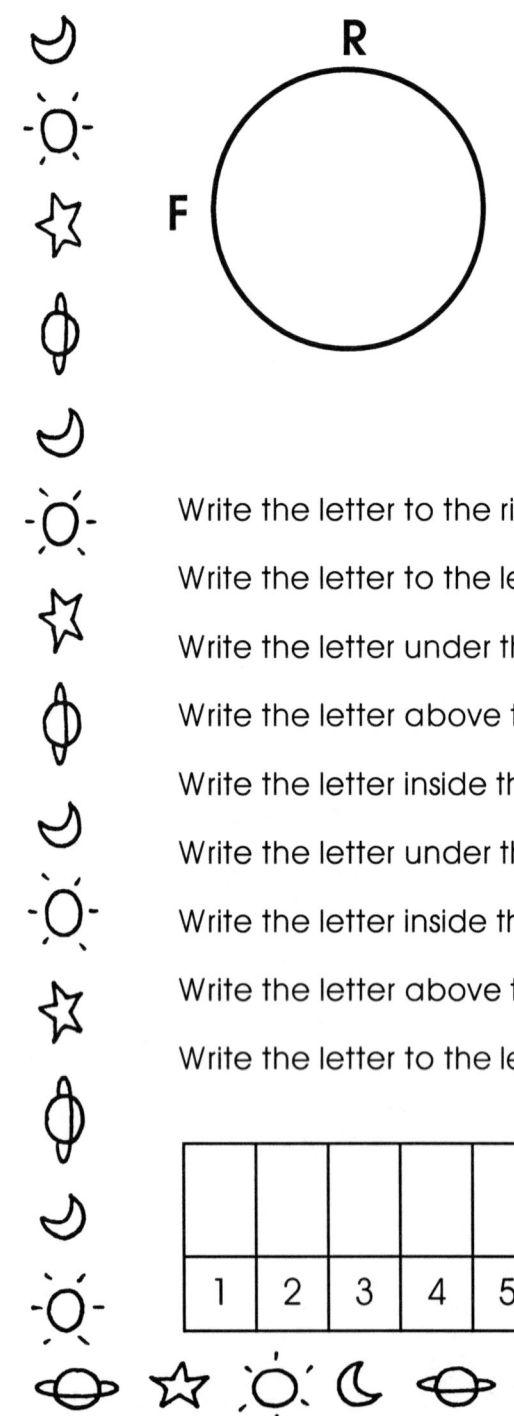

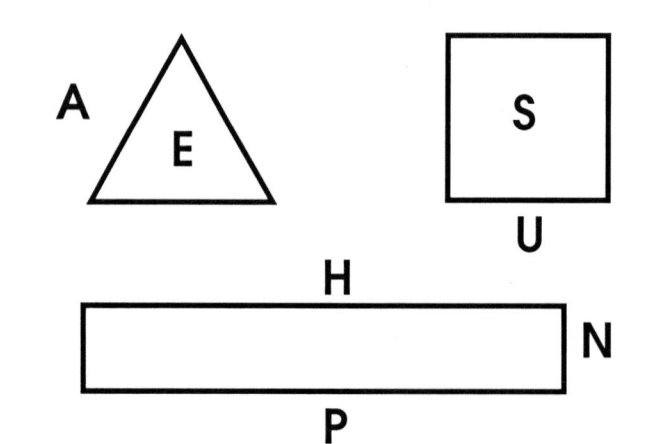

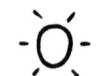

_____ _____
_____ _____

R
A
S
F E U
H
N
P

Write the letter to the right of the rectangle in box 12.

Write the letter to the left of the triangle in boxes 3 and 7.

Write the letter under the rectangle in box 4.

Write the letter above the rectangle in box 2.

Write the letter inside the triangle in boxes 5 and 9.

Write the letter under the square in box 11.

Write the letter inside the square in boxes 1 and 6.

Write the letter above the circle in box 8.

Write the letter to the left of the circle in box 10.

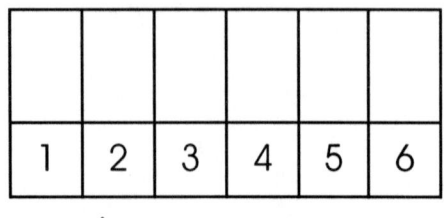

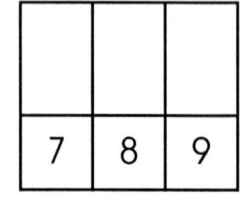

| 1 | 2 | 3 | 4 | 5 | 6 | | 7 | 8 | 9 | | 10 | 11 | 12 |

Creative Thinking in Science

**CREATIVE THINKING
Science
ACTIVITIES**

Theme: Pets

Fluency

- Ask pupils to list all the animals they have as pets.
- Ask pupils to name five animals that are extinct. What are five questions you would have liked to ask one of the extinct animals?
- Ask children which animals make the best pets? Why?
- Pupils can list the different types of food that their pets eat.
- Ask pupils to list animals that would not make good pets. Why?

Flexibility

- Ask pupils to work out three different ways to clean a dirty dog without using water.
- What common points can pupils think of between a mouse and a cup of coffee?
- Say: 'Convince your parents that a hippopotamus would make a great pet.'
- Classify the list of pets into big and little. Ask pupils to group them in other ways.
- Say: 'Do you think animals can talk to each other? Observe a group of animals. What sounds do they make? What do you think the sounds mean? How could you talk to animals?'
- Ask pupils what the pros and cons are of being a kangaroo.
- Pupils can compare a polar bear with a squirrel. How are they similar? How are they different?

Originality

- Ask pupils how they could hide an elephant.
- Say: 'You have lots of pet mice to give away. Think of ways to convince people that mice would make the best pets in the world.'
- Ask pupils to pretend that they are a goldfish and describe what life is like inside a goldfish bowl.
- Say: 'If all the animals decided to rule the world, which animal would be the leader? Why?'
- Plan a *Pet Day* for the class. Ask pupils to work in groups allocated to planning different sections of the day, for example: the timetable, the list of pets, invitations.

Elaboration

- Ask pupils to decide which would be the best animal to have as a class pet. Ask them to justify their choices.
- Ask: 'What if you had a broken leg and couldn't take your dog for a walk? How many other ways could you exercise it?'
- Ask pupils to say whether they would rather be a giraffe or a green tree frog and give reasons for their answers.
- Say 'If you could be any animal in the world, which animal would you choose? Give at least five reasons for your choice.'

Creative Thinking in Science

A Different Dog Kennel

Draw a dog kennel.

Can you make it different by:

Making one part bigger?

Adding something extra?

Replacing one part with something else?

Pet Goldfish

Can you design a collar for a goldfish?

My Pet Shark

Sharks would make excellent pets.

List three good points and three bad points for this idea.

An Ideal Pet

Create an animal that can fly, swim, walk, climb, carry you for long distances and would make an ideal pet.

Name:

Management Strategies: ▼ → ●

CREATIVE THINKING
Science
Worksheet 15

Life in a Goldfish Bowl

My name is _____

I am a _____

I eat _____

The good things about living in a goldfish bowl.

_____
_____
_____
_____
_____
_____
_____

The bad things about living in a goldfish bowl.

_____
_____
_____
_____
_____
_____
_____

One day something terrible happened to me . . .

_____
_____
_____
_____

Brilliant Publications   Thinking Strategies for the Successful Classroom, 5–7 Year Olds   43

Research Skills

by **Rosalind Curtis**

Overview for the Classroom Teacher

RESEARCH SKILLS NOTES

Research Skills

Research skills are needed by all pupils so that they can analyse and interpret information that is presented to them. Information can be presented to pupils by means of written text, pictures, videos, computer terminal, aural input (listening to speakers, radio, sounds within the environment) and the senses of touch, taste and smell.

Research skills that need to be taught to pupils are:

Questioning Techniques to help pupils clarify issues, problems and decisions when looking at a topic.

Developing Planning Frameworks that will assist pupils to access prior knowledge and identify sources of information which will help build further knowledge and understanding.

Gathering Strategies to help pupils collect and store information for later consideration (for example note taking, identifying main ideas and text clarification).

Sorting Strategies that help pupils to prioritize and organize information (for example by using retrieval charts and sequencing information).

Synthesizing Skills help the pupil to take the original information and reorganize it in order to develop decisions and solutions.

Evaluation helps the pupil to determine if the information found is sufficient to support a solution or conclusion.

Reporting Skills allow the pupil to translate findings into a persuasive, instructive and effective product, for example in the presentation of a project.

These research skills are best taught within the classroom by means of a **Research Cycle**. This cycle provides pupils with the steps to plan and conduct meaningful research to complete projects, solve problems and make informed decisions.

① Pupils **explore** a variety of sources to gather information.

② Pupils **identify** information sources that will contain data to help with their decision.

③ Once information is found, **decisions** must be made about which data to keep.

④ Pupils **sort** information to enable them to categorize and organize their findings so that analysis can begin.

⑤ Pupils begin to **analyse** their data by establishing criteria that will help them reach a decision.

⑥ Pupils **ask** themselves why this information is important and how it will affect their decision.

⑦ After completion of analysis, pupils will **combine** their findings to create their final project.

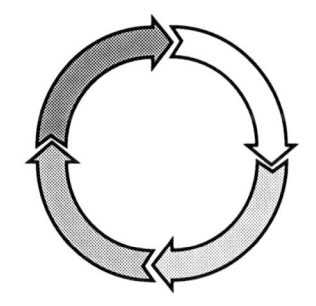

Brilliant Publications — Thinking Strategies for the Successful Classroom, 5–7 Year Olds

RESEARCH SKILLS NOTES

Overview for the Classroom Teacher

The Research Cycle

There are seven steps in the Research Cycle.

1 Questioning

- This step identifies the problem that needs solving.
- Pupils need to be taught questioning skills that will enable them to identify what data is needed to solve the main problem. It is critical pupils are encouraged to think laterally and from as many perspectives as possible.
- From the questioning process, pupils should be able to identify information they already know and formulate questions to locate information they need to find out.

2 Planning

- This step begins to develop information-seeking strategies to help locate answers to all the questions asked.
- Pupils need to be introduced to the range of resources that are available, such as books, videos, people, pictures and the Internet.
- Pupils need to plan how to organize the information that will be gathered.

3 Gathering

- This step enables pupils to clarify the information that has been located.
- Pupils need to develop effective note-taking strategies so that the main idea is identified from the information.
- Pupils also need to recognize the value of a bibliography so that they may return to an information source if required.

4 Sorting

- This step requires pupils to systematically scan the data for relevant information that will contribute to understanding.
- Pupils need to classify the gathered information under headings and sub-headings and make generalizations about it.
- The data gathered could then be placed into a sequence of events.

5 Synthesizing

- This process is like doing a jigsaw puzzle.
- Pupils need to arrange and rearrange fragments of information until patterns begin to emerge.
- Pupils develop their skills so that they are able to answer questions with understanding, accuracy and detail.

6 Evaluation

- When this stage is first reached, early attempts to synthesize information may result in the need for more information to clarify or enhance understanding. If the pupils find that pieces are missing, they will need to begin the cycle again or ask what more is needed to complete their picture.
- As the cycle begins again, questioning will become more specific and will lead to more planning and more gathering of information.
- When the picture seems to be complete, the pupils can decide that the cycle should finish.
- It may be necessary to repeat the cycle and gather more information until the pupils decide that the investigation is complete.

7 Reporting

- After the cycle has been completed, it is time to report and share findings. This may take the form of an oral, written or graphic presentation, a debate or any other presentation that pupils may decide upon.

Classroom Design

- Have pupils work independently or in mixed-ability or homogeneous groups as appropriate to the activity.
- Provide a variety of resources around the room, including hands-on and extension activities, and learning/interest centres (see page 8) aimed at different levels.
- Always give criteria for marking and a time schedule for work to be completed.

Research Skills in Literacy

Theme: Health and Sport

Questioning

- Show pupils a picture of a sportsperson. Encourage them to ask questions like:
    - What is this person doing? (Factual)
    - What did this person do to win the event? (Inferential)
    - If this person is a member of a team, what did they have to do to win? (Creative)
    - Do you think this person could have performed better on the day? Why? (Critical)
- Ask pupils to devise questions to find out the class's favourite food.

Planning

- Ask pupils to write down different sources of information about food (for example cookery books, magazines, recipe cards).
- Identify words that could be used to search on the Internet for a sport (tennis, Wimbledon, Andy Murray) or food (health, recipes, diet).
- Model a mind map on the board. (A mind map is a diagram that features words and ideas relating to and arranged around a central concept.) Ask pupils to draw their own mind map for a sport.

Gathering

- Ask pupils to bring in newspapers, magazines or catalogues containing pictures of sports equipment, sports- people and different types of food.
- Show pupils a video of famous sports-people and then ask them to draw or write down important facts about the person.
- Ask children to list a variety of different manufactured health foods such as muesli bars and cereals.
- Allow pupils to visit websites such as **www.uksport.gov.uk** to locate sporting information.

Sorting

- Model how to sort foods according to different attributes like snack food and wholesome food. Ask pupils to categorize the foods in as many different ways as possible, for example: carbohydrates, fruit, dairy food.
- Ask children to organize information under headings in their sports mind maps so that they can identify data which is important to them.

Synthesizing

- Ask pupils to use the information they have gathered to help them identify the important elements of being a good sportsperson, for example, having a healthy diet.
- Ask children to draw a cartoon strip about how a particular sportsperson became famous.
- Pupils can role-play this person performing a winning moment in their sport.

Evaluating

- Encourage pupils to give reasons why a particular food is good for them.
- Ask pupils to choose their favourite sportsperson. Ask them to explain why they think their particular person is better than any other famous sportsperson.
- Ask pupils to write a recipe using their favourite food. Is this food healthy?

Reporting

- Pupils can present a one-minute oral report to convince the class that their favourite sportsperson is the greatest ever.
- Ask pupils to write a story or use pictures to tell about meeting their famous sportsperson.
- Ask them to write a jingle about their favourite healthy food.

RESEARCH SKILLS
Literacy
Worksheet 16

Name:

Food

Management Strategies:

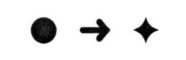

● → ✦

Sorting, Analysing

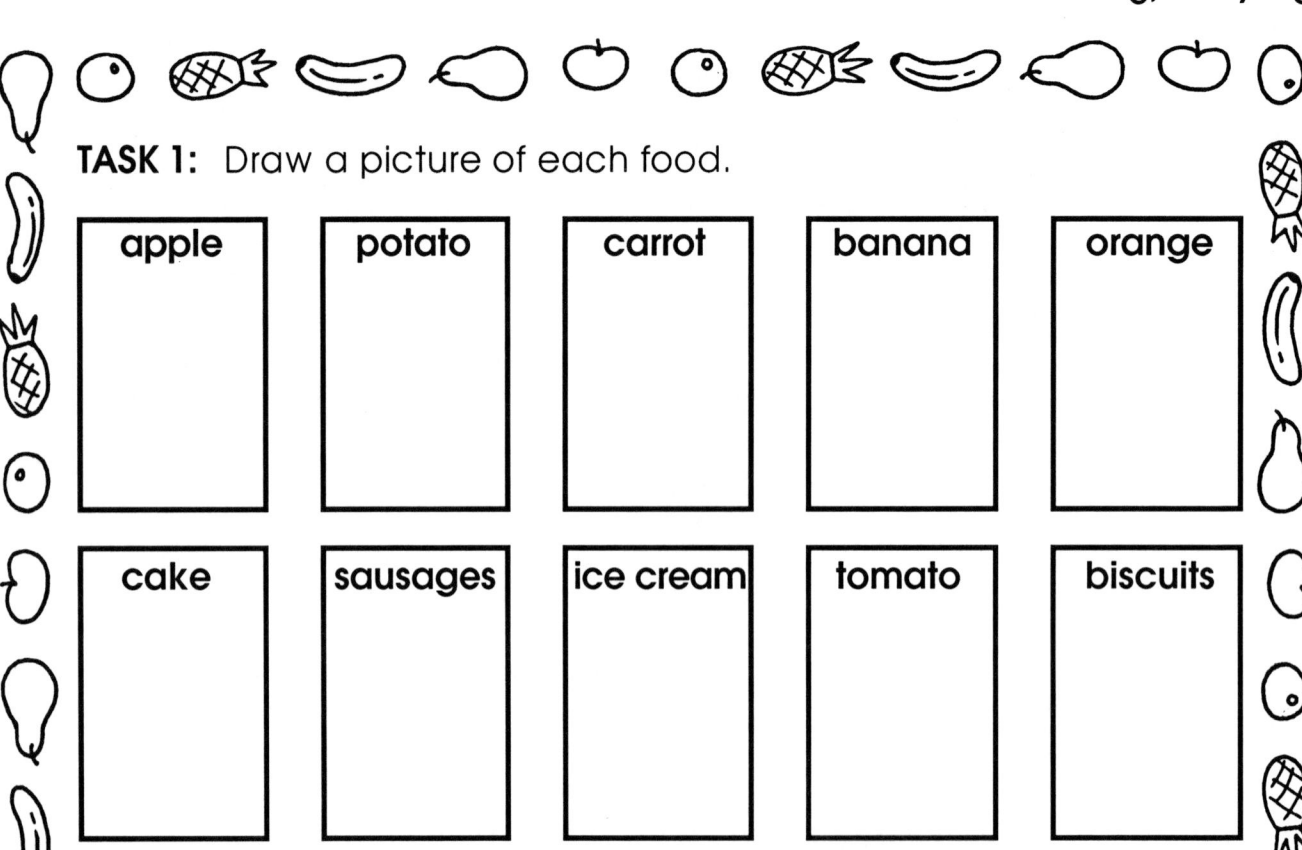

TASK 1: Draw a picture of each food.

apple	potato	carrot	banana	orange

cake	sausages	ice cream	tomato	biscuits

TASK 2: Sort these foods into different groups (for example sweet food, snack food, healthy food).

Sweet Food	Snack Food	Healthy Food

48   Thinking Strategies for the Successful Classroom, 5–7 Year Olds   Brilliant Publications

This page may be photocopied for use by the purchasing institution only.
© Blake Education Pty Ltd. 2004

Name: _____

Management Strategies:

RESEARCH SKILLS
Literacy
Worksheet 17

Famous Sportspeople

Synthesizing, Evaluating

1. Find a picture of a famous sportsperson and glue it here.
   Write some facts about this person.

   Name: _____

   Sport: _____

   Sport equipment used: _____

2. If you were to meet this person, what are two questions you would like to ask them?

   (a) _____

   _____

   (b) _____

   _____

3. List four skills you would need to be good at this sport. Draw pictures of yourself practising these skills.

Skill:	Skill:
Skill:	Skill:

Brilliant Publications Thinking Strategies for the Successful Classroom, 5–7 Year Olds

Research Skills in Maths

Theme: Numeration

Questioning

- Ask pupils questions about how numbers are written, such as:
  - What do we call the symbols that we use to count with?
  - How is the position of each number important?
  - What does 437 mean? Can I write it in a different way?
- Encourage pupils to identify different words related to numeration, such as place value, ones, tens, hundreds. Ask them to explain how these relate to the way numbers are represented.

Planning

- Ask children to verbalize the steps they will take in deciding how to represent a number with a group of counters or a bundle of sticks.
- Ask pupils how place value could be represented in a number like 621.
- Encourage pupils to write down or verbalize any information or processes they already know that could help them solve a problem. For example: 'I know that 16 can be written as 1 ten and 6 ones.'

Gathering

- Ask pupils to try all the different ways that they can think of to represent 999.
- Pupils can compare different answers to the same problem. For example:
  $3 + 3 = 4 + 2 = 5 + 1 = 7 - 1$.
- Ask pupils to find pictures to represent the same numbers (a picture with 5 dogs, a sentence with 5 words, 5 tally marks).

Sorting

- Ask pupils to arrange numbers in ascending and descending order.
- Ask pupils to arrange a group of numbers such as 48, 4, 473 and 41 from lowest to highest.

Synthesizing

- How many different ways can pupils find to represent numbers (for example pictures, symbols or different number sentences)?
- Ask children to develop patterns using place value and repetition of number patterns.
- Pupils can devise problems for the rest of the class to solve using numeration. For example: 'Is 51 higher than 510?'

Evaluating

- Ask pupils to check if given answers to an algorithm have correct place value and explain why.
- Give pupils some information and ask them to explain if it is correct or incorrect. Let them give reasons for their decisions. For example: 'Is 327 made up of 3 tens, 2 hundreds and 7 ones?'

Reporting

- Ask pupils to present an oral report on how they went about solving a problem. Make sure that they verbalize all steps taken and give reasons for why they solved the problem in that particular way.
- Pupils can present a dramatization of a number sentence such as 'Three birds sitting on a tree, two more joined them and that made five'.

Name:

Management Strategies:

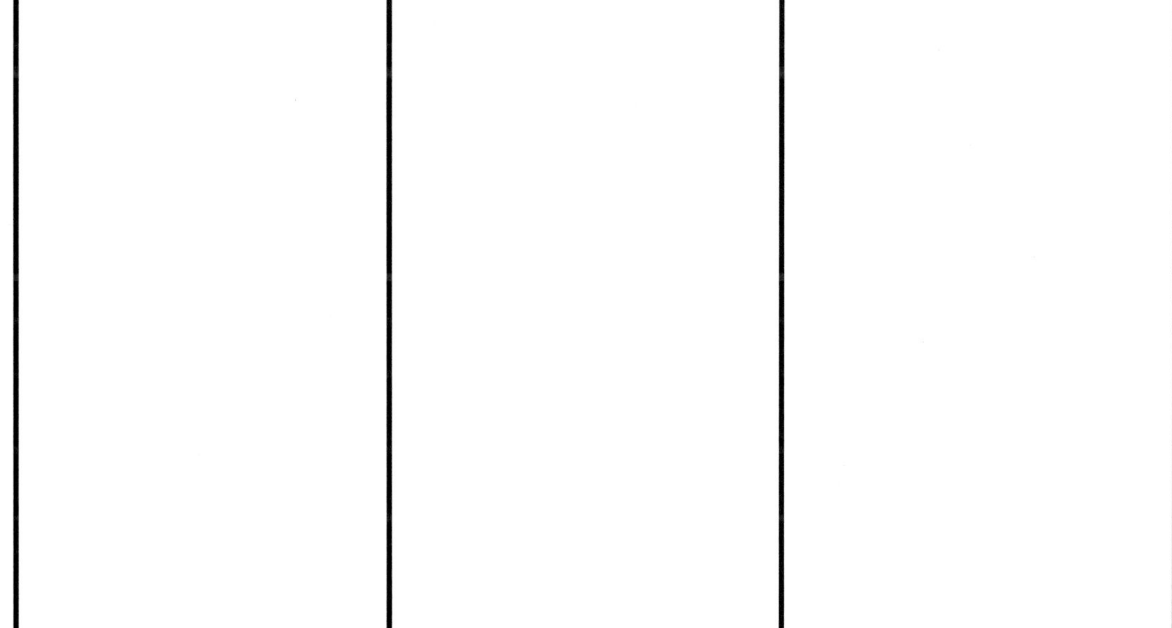

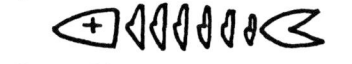

RESEARCH SKILLS
Maths
Worksheet 18

Representing Numbers

Locating Information, Sorting, Analysing

We can represent the number 12 using pictures and number sentences:

12 ✸✸✸✸✸✸✸✸✸✸ ✸✸	12 ❀❀❀❀ ☆☆☆☆ ❄❄❄❄
10 + 2	4 + 4 + 4

Think of two more ways to represent the number 12.

12	12

TASK: Use pictures and number sentences to represent the numbers 11, 15 and 18 in as many different ways as you can.

11	15	18

RESEARCH SKILLS Maths TASK CARDS

Research Skills in Maths

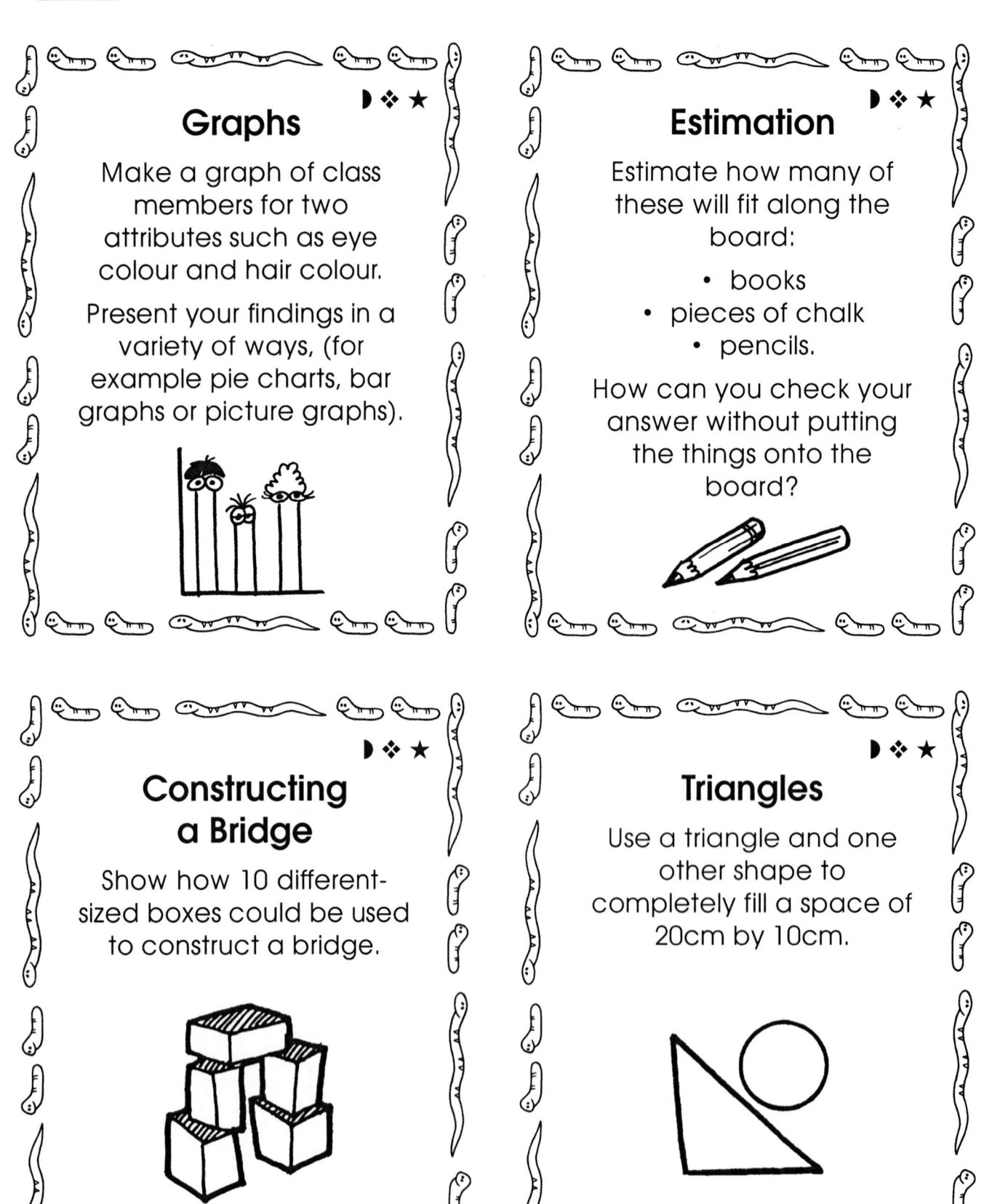

Graphs ◗ ❖ ★

Make a graph of class members for two attributes such as eye colour and hair colour.

Present your findings in a variety of ways, (for example pie charts, bar graphs or picture graphs).

Estimation ◗ ❖ ★

Estimate how many of these will fit along the board:
- books
- pieces of chalk
- pencils.

How can you check your answer without putting the things onto the board?

Constructing a Bridge ◗ ❖ ★

Show how 10 different-sized boxes could be used to construct a bridge.

Triangles ◗ ❖ ★

Use a triangle and one other shape to completely fill a space of 20cm by 10cm.

Research Skills in Humanities

Theme: Toys and Games

Questioning

- Encourage pupils to question given statements such as:
  - 'We need toys to help us learn.'
  - 'Toys are better today than when our parents were children.'
- Ask pupils to devise the questions that go with given answers. For example:
  - 'If the answer is *Snakes and Ladders*, what could the question be?'
- Let pupils make up questions for surveys to gauge opinions on using electronic games versus board games.

Planning

- Ask pupils to identify those resources that could hold information for further research into toys and games (books, toy stores, grandparents, Internet).
- Ask children to write down what information they know and what they wish to find out about toys and games, such as indoor games, outdoor games or materials used to make toys.

Gathering

- Let pupils select a game or toy and write down what they think are the good and bad points.
- Ask pupils to bring in books, magazines and pictures of a variety of toys so that they can examine many different types.
- Allow pupils to visit websites such as **www.bbc.co.uk/history/forkids** to find out about the history of toys and games.

Sorting

- Collect different types of wheels, feet, wings and springs that can be found on toys and sort them according to various attributes such as size, shape and usefulness.
- Give pupils a list of games and ask them to rank them from most to least enjoyable.
- Ask pupils to match games and rules. For example 'rugby' with 'try'.

Synthesizing

- Ask pupils to write a letter to a friend describing a new toy.
- Ask pupils for suggestions of how to improve a game.
- Ask pupils to devise a new toy.

Evaluating

- Ask pupils to explain why they think their new toy will be better than any other toy.
- Ask pupils to give reasons for their choices and to explain why they will work.
- Ask pupils to comment on other pupils' toys and to state whether they would buy them.

Reporting

- Ask pupils to write an advertisement for their new toy.
- Pupils can give an oral or written report on their toy. The purpose of the report is to persuade people to buy the toy.
- As a major activity, pupils can design their ideal new school. Encourage them to present their schools in the form of models.

RESEARCH SKILLS — Humanities — Worksheet 19

Name: _____

Management Strategies: ★ ☽ ❖ ▼

A New Toy

Sorting, Evaluating

Develop a new toy that has wheels, wings, feet and springs.

In the spaces below, write how many of each item your toy will have and draw what each part will look like.

Wheels	Wings	Feet	Springs

My toy will be called: _____

This is what my toy can do: _____

_____

_____

Draw how you and your friends could use this toy.

The best thing about this toy is: _____

_____

54 — Thinking Strategies for the Successful Classroom, 5–7 Year Olds — Brilliant Publications

This page may be photocopied for use by the purchasing institution only. © Blake Education Pty Ltd. 2004

Name: _____

Management Strategies:
★ ◆ ✦ ⟲

RESEARCH SKILLS
Humanities
Worksheet 20

A Different School

Gathering, Synthesizing, Evaluating

Design a new school. You can decide what the school will be called and what type of lessons are to be taught.

My new school will be called _____

This is what my new school will look like

Lessons to be taught	When?

I would like these lessons because _____
_____
_____
_____

Three important school rules will be:

1 _____
2 _____
3 _____

Brilliant Publications — Thinking Strategies for the Successful Classroom, 5–7 Year Olds

Questioning Skills and Brainstorming

by **Fay Holbert**

Overview for the Classroom Teacher

QUESTION/BRAINSTORM NOTES

Questioning Skills and Brainstorming

Generally speaking, 30% of class time is taken up in questioning (that is about 100 questions per hour). In most classrooms, 85% of questions are asked by the teacher, and 90% of those do no more than demand memory or recall by the pupils! Therefore, teachers should aim to use more open-ended and divergent questions to improve the pupils' creative thinking and problem-solving abilities.

Questioning Guidelines for the Teacher:

1. Maintain a high level of enthusiasm.
2. Accept that individual differences in pupils will determine how, what, how much and how fast learning occurs.
3. Encourage divergent thinking.
4. Avoid all forms of 'put-downs'. Be positive! Say: 'Great!' 'Good try!' 'Tell me more!' 'I've never thought of it like that!'
5. Try to minimize 'Who?' 'What?' 'Where?' and maximize 'Why?' 'How?'

Bloom's Taxonomy emphasizes the idea that with brighter pupils, more time should be devoted to the higher-level activities and objectives. *Knowledge* and *Comprehension* deal with facts, figures, definitions and rules that all pupils need to know. However, teachers should encourage the brighter pupils (who will generally grasp new information quickly and comprehend more rapidly) to:

◆ *Apply* this knowledge.

◆ *Analyse* components, relationships and hypotheses.

◆ *Synthesize* these components into creative solutions, plans and theories.

◆ *Evaluate* the accuracy, value and efficiency of alternative ideas or actions.

Examples of Questions That Help to Apply Knowledge:

When did ... ?

Can you list ... ?

Which action/event was the cause of ... ?

Can you give an example of ... ?

How would you have ... ?

Why was ... ?

Examples of Questions That Help to Analyse Knowledge:

Why did ... do this?

Can you sequence ... ?

Examples of Questions That Help to Synthesize Knowledge:

How would this situation have changed if ... ?

What if the ... had been ... ?

Examples of Questions That Help to Evaluate the Knowledge:

How could ... have been improved?

Who do you think has the strongest character? Why?

Brilliant Publications — Thinking Strategies for the Successful Classroom, 5–7 Year Olds

Overview for the Classroom Teacher

Brainstorming

Another questioning technique, that encourages creative thinking is **brainstorming.**

The aim of brainstorming is to develop a safe, non-judgemental setting where all pupils feel confident and eager to participate in the lesson.

It was Alex Osborn who identified some valuable conditions and rules for brainstorming. The main principle is *deferred judgement*. This means that idea evaluation is postponed until later. Osborn stressed that any kind of criticism or evaluation interferes with the generation of imaginative ideas, simply because it is very difficult to do both at the same time.

It is important for the teacher to remind the pupils of the basic rules of brainstorming:

1. No criticism is allowed, no matter how irrelevant or preposterous the responses may appear to be.
2. Quantity of ideas is required. The more ideas you have, the more likely it is that you will have motivated all pupils to contribute, and thus it is more likely that you will find good solutions.
3. Accept and record all answers. To begin with, it is perhaps easier for the teacher to be the scribe, but when brainstorming is a regular feature of the class's activities, pupils can record responses.
4. Eliminate any stiffness or inflexibility. Be open to alternatives.
5. If responses slacken off, add your own. The teacher's role is to keep urging: 'What else could we do?' 'Who else has an idea?' The teacher may even specifically direct questions to a group of quieter pupils.
6. Link ideas wherever possible. Ask questions such as: 'How can we express this more clearly?' 'Could we improve this one?' 'What if we put these three ideas together?'
7. Encourage fantasy, imagination and lateral thinking.
8. Encourage co-operative work among pupils.
9. If there were a school problem (for example, the sudden appearance of graffiti in the school playground), the pupils could be given 24-hours' notice so that *all* have an opportunity to discuss this at home and be prepared to brainstorm a solution for the next day. Brighter pupils soon learn to organize and lead group brainstorming sessions.

Some variations of brainstorming are:

Reverse Brainstorming: This technique quickly points out what is currently being done incorrectly and implicitly suggests specific solutions. For example: 'How can we *increase* vandalism?'

'Stop and Go' Brainstorming: Short periods of approximately 6–8 minutes of brainstorming are interspersed with evaluation. The evaluation sheets help keep the group on target by selecting the most profitable directions to pursue.

Phillips 66: This is a technique using small groups of 6. Pupils brainstorm for 6 minutes and then a member of each group reports the best (or all) ideas to the larger group.

Questioning Skills and Brainstorming in Literacy

Theme: People Who Help in the Community

Knowledge

- Hold a teacher-led discussion to ascertain that all pupils understand the concept of a community.
- Brainstorm:
  - What is a community? What makes up a community?
  - List some important people who help make your community a better and safer place too live.
  - Find out how many pupils know the emergency services telephone number (999). Write this number in the classroom in an obvious location for all to see and memorize.

Comprehension

- Ask pupils what they understand by the term 'emergency call'.
- Ask: 'How can you tell when the emergency services are responding to an emergency call?'
- From the brainstorming list of 'Important people in our community', have pupils identify the ones who help us to save lives.
- Ask: 'Why do these people need fast vehicles?'
- Brainstorm: 'How do police officers help us? How do paramedics help us? How do firefighters help us?'

Application

- Give pupils several emergency scenarios, such as their house being on fire. Ask them how they would react in each circumstance.
- Put pupils in groups of four to five to role-play the rescuers and rescued in some of these emergency scenarios.
- Ask the question: 'Are there differences between the sirens that the police, ambulance and fire vehicles use? Why?'

Analysis

- Ask: 'Can you list the skills that a police officer, a paramedic and a firefighter would need to be able to perform their duties well?'
- Brainstorm: 'How can you avoid accidents that need the attention of these people?'
- Ask: 'Why do you think uniforms are worn by these people while they are on duty?'
- Ask the pupils to list the many different types of duties that the above three community helpers are called upon to perform. For example, the police may catch criminals, look for missing persons, or present talks at schools.

Synthesis

Ask questions such as:

- What would you do if paramedics were already busy at a major emergency when you rang for them to come? Who else could you call for help?
- What happens to people who live in small, remote communities when they are in need of urgent medical help? Ask pupils to choose some of these scenarios to role-play.
- How could you help police officers, paramedics and firefighters to do their jobs? How can we get to know more about the work that these people do?
- Plan a display of 'People Who Help in Our Community' for the classroom or school library. Pupils can design posters and collect pictures, brochures and newspaper articles to display that show how each of these organizations is structured.

Evaluation

- Ask: 'What would it be like to have none of these men and women available to us for a whole day?'
- List ways that people in our community show their appreciation for the work that these people do, (for example writing to thank them for their hard work in the community).
- Is there anything more that people could do to assist/improve these organizations?
- Organize excursions to your local police, ambulance and fire stations.

QUESTION/ BRAINSTORM
Literacy
Worksheet 21

Name:

People Who Help in the Community

Management Strategies:
▼ ✱
✖ ♣

Application, Synthesis

TASK 1: Draw some of the equipment these community helpers use.

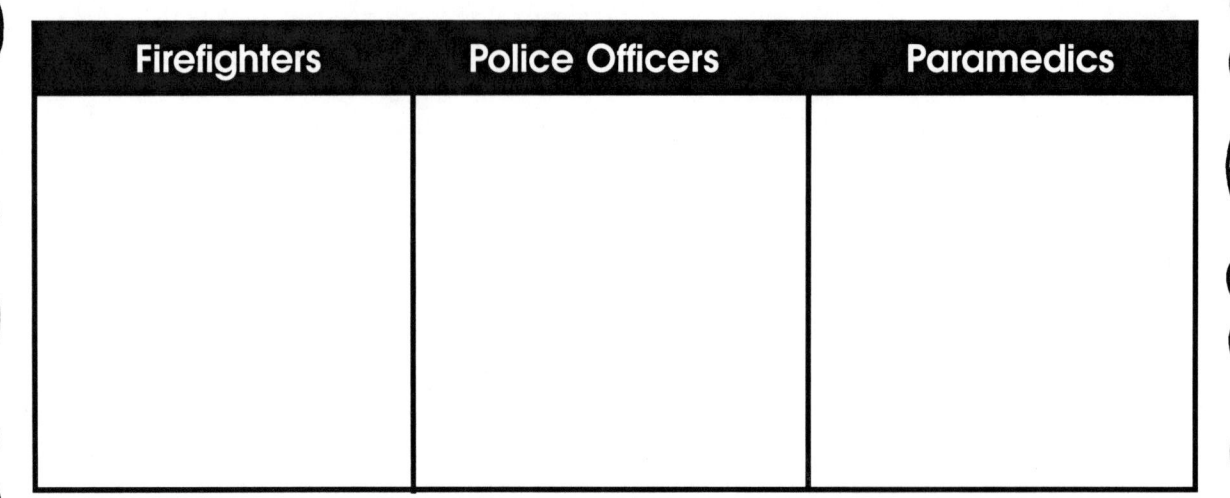

Firefighters	Police Officers	Paramedics

TASK 2: Draw an emergency where all three of the above community helpers have been called upon to work together.

TASK 3: Describe what has happened.

_____
_____
_____
_____

Questioning Skills and Brainstorming in Literacy

Application, Analysis, Evaluation

Asking Questions

Prepare three interesting questions you would like to ask the staff at your local:

- Police Station
- Fire Station
- Hospital

Road Rules

Work in a small group to set up a 'busy junction' in your school playground.

Take turns to act as pedestrians, cyclists, car drivers and police officers to make sure that everyone knows road and safety rules.

Shortest Route

On a map of your town community, use different colours to trace the shortest routes that you could take to drive from home to:

- the Hospital
- the Police Station
- the Fire Station.

The Future

Design new tools and vehicles that each of our community helpers might be able to use in the future.

Draw diagrams of your inventions with labels for their parts. Explain how your inventions would work.

QUESTION/ BRAINSTORM Maths ACTIVITIES

Questioning Skills and Brainstorming in Maths

Theme: Shapes

Introduction

- Display diagrams of shapes, such as squares, triangles (equilateral, isosceles, scalene), rectangles, hexagons and diamonds.

- Write the above words on the board. Also add: straight, curved, parallel, round, oval, angle, right angle, quadrilateral. Point to the shapes to help explain each of these features.

Knowledge

- Ask pupils to name the displayed shapes as they are indicated by the teacher.

- Encourage pupils to explain the properties of each shape.

- Ask pupils to write the words on the board to illustrate the new vocabulary they have learned.

Comprehension

- Brainstorm: How many square, triangular, rectangular, circular and hexagonal shapes can you find:
  - in the classroom
  - at home
  - outdoors

- Give pupils examples of the above shapes cut out of card in many different sizes and colours. Ask them to place them in their appropriate groups.

Application

- Ask: 'What could you use to draw a circle?' Pupils can demonstrate their ideas.

- Ask pupils to write the letters of the alphabet under the headings:
  - Letters with straight lines
  - Letters with curved lines
  - Letters with both straight and curved lines.
  - Ask the question: 'How could you form an exact right angle by folding a piece of paper?' Allow pupils to experiment.

Analysis

- Ask: 'What is common to all the above shapes except the circle?' Pupils can work in groups to list suggestions and report back to the class.

- Ask pupils to investigate what makes a square different from:
  - a rectangle
  - any other quadrilateral

- Ask: 'Why is the circle different from all the other shapes?'

Synthesis

To stimulate synthesizing activities, ask open-ended questions such as those listed below, and encourage pupils to experiment:

- What shapes could you draw if you had only a piece of string and a pencil?

- Why is it easier to use a tool that has a round handle rather than a square one?

- What difficulties would we face if we had triangular television screens?

- Why do you think steps are usually rectangular?

Evaluation

- Organize a trip to the local supermarket. Ask pupils to note the most common shapes of goods on the shelves and report their findings back to the class. (They could also use the school canteen as an alternative venue.)

- Ask pupils to find out: 'What is the most common type of line (straight, curved, zigzag) used in constructing a building?'

- Ask the question: 'What are the most common shapes seen in the structure of a house?' Pupils can present an oral or written report to the class on their findings.

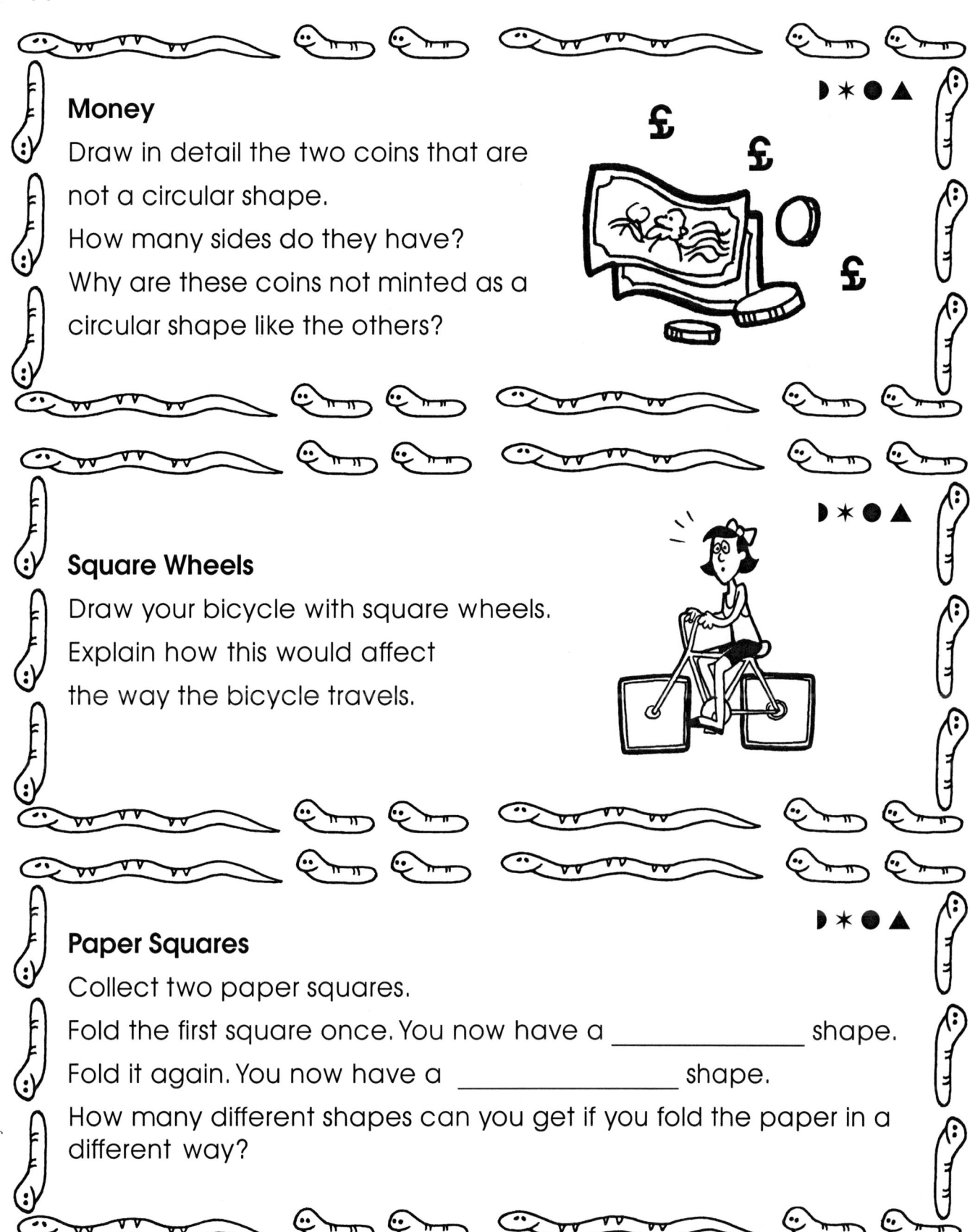

Questioning Skills and Brainstorming in Maths

QUESTION/ BRAINSTORM
Maths
TASK CARDS

Application

Money

Draw in detail the two coins that are not a circular shape.

How many sides do they have?

Why are these coins not minted as a circular shape like the others?

Square Wheels

Draw your bicycle with square wheels. Explain how this would affect the way the bicycle travels.

Paper Squares

Collect two paper squares.

Fold the first square once. You now have a _____ shape.

Fold it again. You now have a _____ shape.

How many different shapes can you get if you fold the paper in a different way?

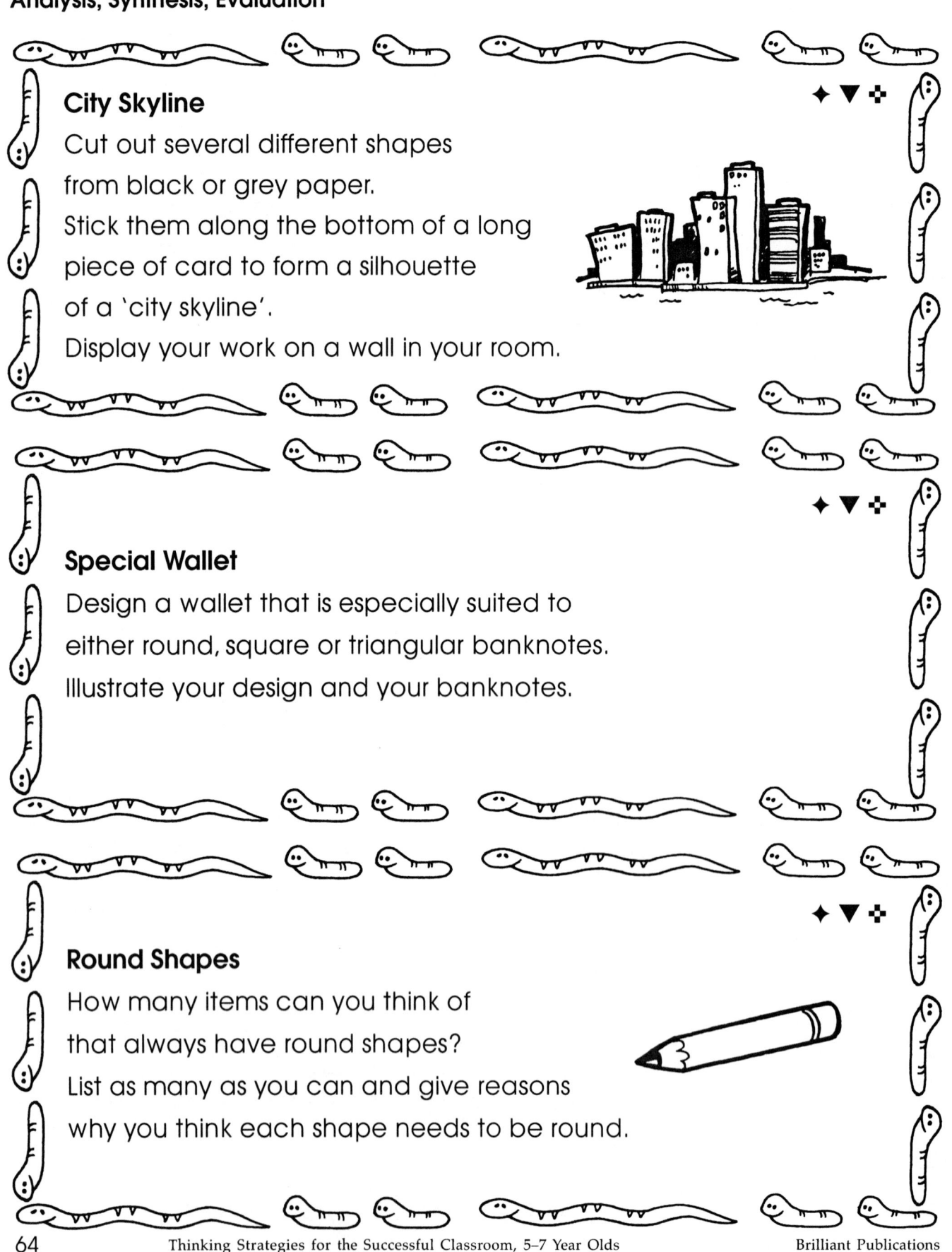

Questioning Skills and Brainstorming in Maths

Analysis, Synthesis, Evaluation

City Skyline

Cut out several different shapes from black or grey paper. Stick them along the bottom of a long piece of card to form a silhouette of a 'city skyline'.
Display your work on a wall in your room.

Special Wallet

Design a wallet that is especially suited to either round, square or triangular banknotes. Illustrate your design and your banknotes.

Round Shapes

How many items can you think of that always have round shapes?
List as many as you can and give reasons why you think each shape needs to be round.

Questioning Skills and Brainstorming in Science

Theme: The Skeleton

Introduction

◆ Display a picture of a human skeleton for pupils to identify, to ensure that they are *all* comfortable with the term.

Knowledge

◆ Say: 'Name any bones of the skeleton and point to the bone you name on the diagram of the skeleton.' (For this age group 'shin', 'upper arm', 'ribs' are acceptable.)

◆ Reverse brainstorm with pupils: 'What would happen if we didn't have a skeleton?' Its importance should quickly become clear.

◆ Ask: 'Which bones are often broken by children? Why is this so?'

◆ Ask: 'What are joints? What do our joints do?' Encourage pupils to name all their joints and investigate their flexibility of movement.

Comprehension

◆ Brainstorm: 'What special work do the skull and the ribs do for us?'

◆ Tell the children to look at their hands. Ask: 'How many bones do you think there are in your hand? (27) How many in each finger (4) and thumb (3)?'

◆ Ask the question: 'Which other joints in your body operate like your fingers?' Compare this with the action of a hinge on a door. Encourage pupils to name other similar objects.

◆ Ask: 'Which joints can you name that do not work like hinges? Why is this difference necessary?'

Application

◆ Prepare shapes made from thick card of the main sections of the skeleton, such as the skull, ribcage, arms, legs, pelvis and spine. Ask pupils to reassemble the skeleton using blu-tac®, fine wire and split pins.

◆ Ask the following questions:
   - 'Why do we need so many bones?'
   - 'What can we do to help strengthen our bones?'
   - 'How are you able to move your arms, legs, head?'
   - 'Why do we have skin to cover our skeletons?'

Analysis

Encourage pupils to analyse with questions such as:

   - 'What would happen if we had just one long bone in our leg or arm or back?'
   - 'Why do we need so many bones in our wrists and hands, ankles and feet?'
   - 'What happens when a person breaks a bone? How is it treated? How long does it take to mend?' Encourage pupils to recount any personal experiences with broken bones.

Synthesis

◆ Encourage pupils to find out what equipment is available to help protect their bones while they play sport. What sports do they play where it is advisable to wear this protective equipment?

◆ Ask: 'In what ways are skeletons of other creatures similar to or different from the human skeleton?' Have them compare and contrast the skeletons of a variety of land and sea creatures, for example, a snake (which has only vertebrae), a worm (which has no bones), or a crab (which has its 'skeleton' on the outside).

Evaluation

◆ Ask pupils to make a list of all sports where protective equipment should be compulsory for all players to wear. Ask them to provide reasons for their choices.

◆ Ask: 'How could we make games safer for young people to play?'

◆ Invite a nurse, doctor or paramedic to speak to your class about the human skeleton. Encourage pupils to prepare a list of questions to ask.

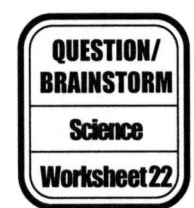

The Human Skeleton

In the boxes below, draw the bones of:
  a) the arm and hand
  b) the leg and foot

Choose the correct words from those below to label each bone and joint:

Forearm (Radius and Ulna)	Upper Arm (Humerus)
Lower Leg (Tibia and Fibula)	Thigh (Femur)
Kneecap (Patella)	Wrist
Ankle	Knee
Elbow	Knuckles

Arm and Hand	Leg and Foot

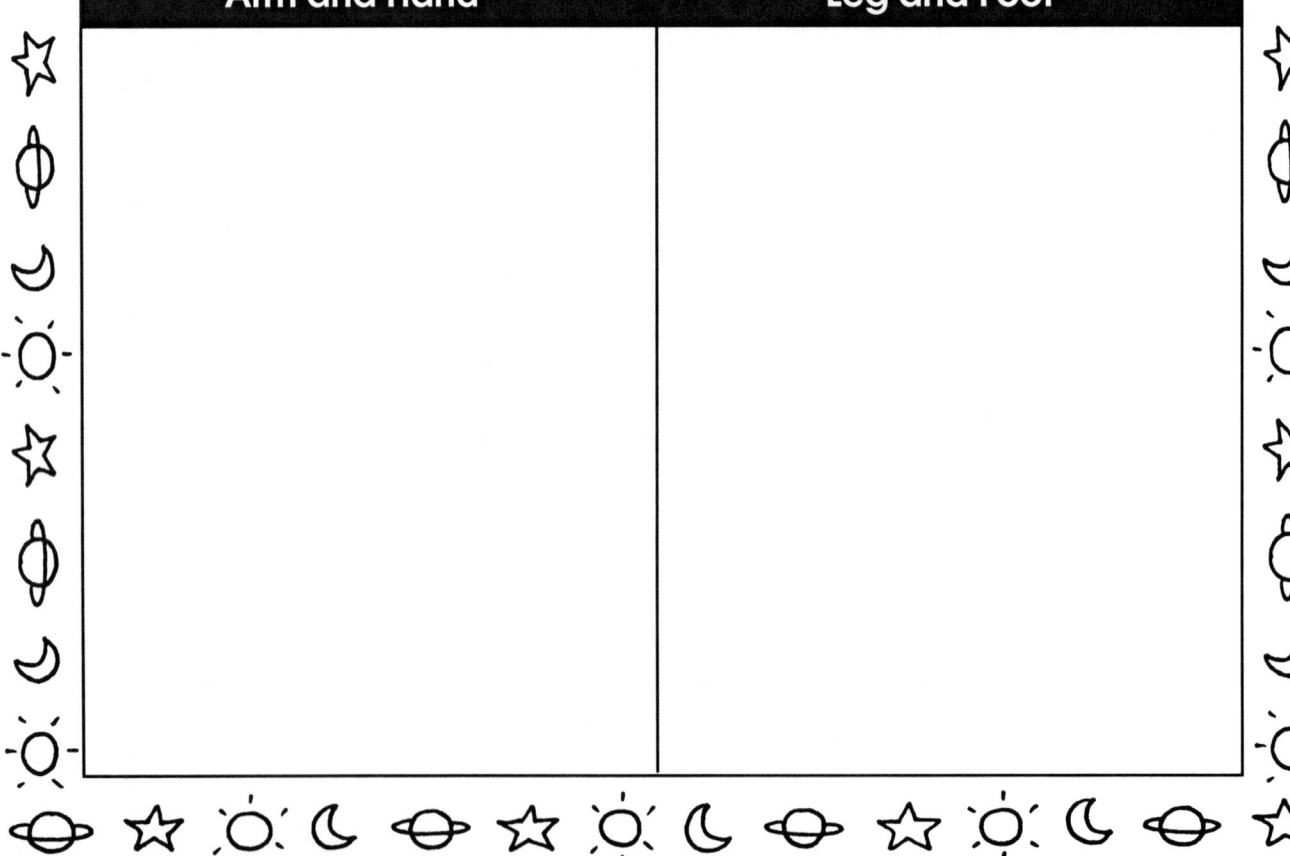

Questioning Skills and Brainstorming in Science

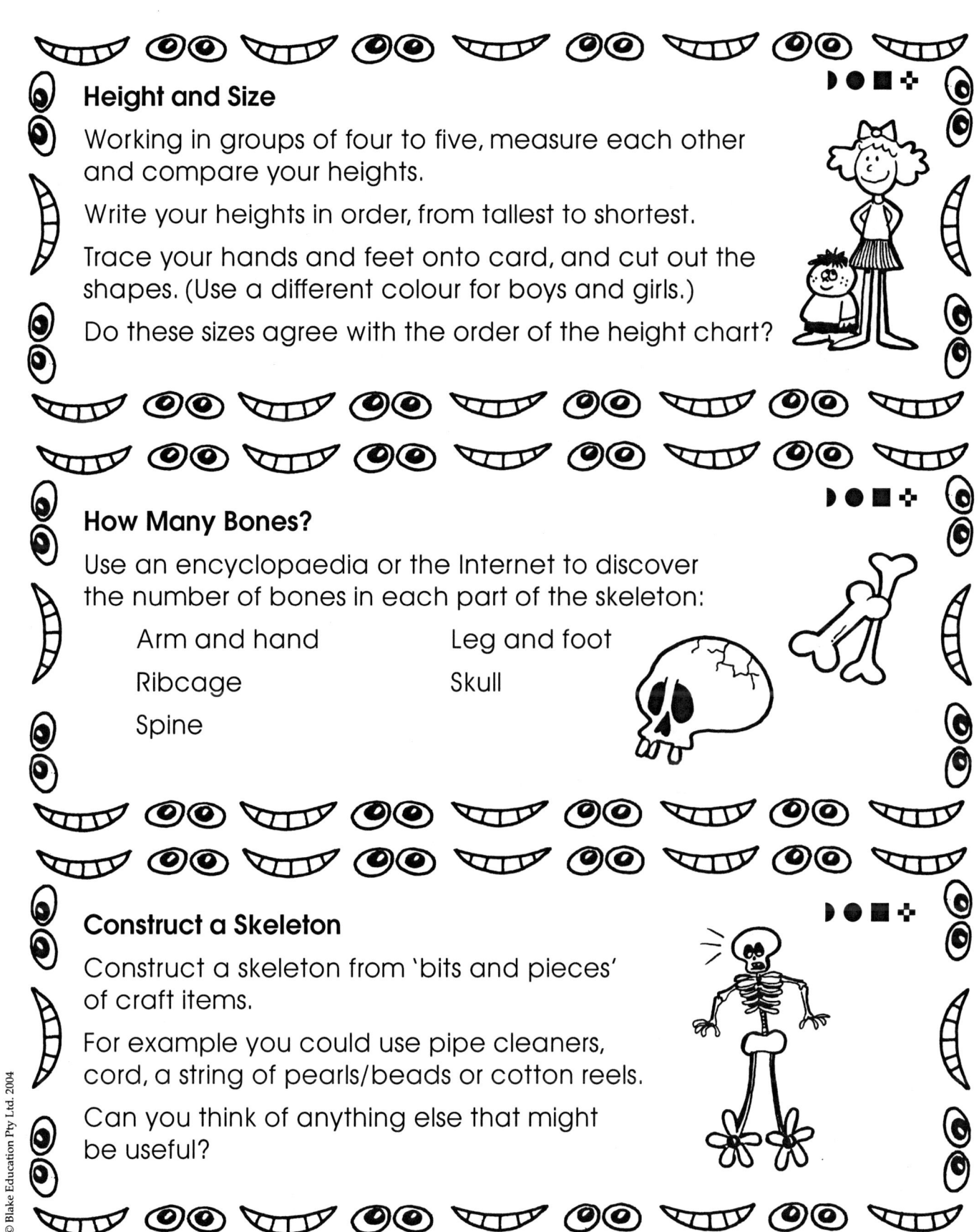

QUESTION/ BRAINSTORM
Science
TASK CARDS

Height and Size

Working in groups of four to five, measure each other and compare your heights.

Write your heights in order, from tallest to shortest.

Trace your hands and feet onto card, and cut out the shapes. (Use a different colour for boys and girls.)

Do these sizes agree with the order of the height chart?

How Many Bones?

Use an encyclopaedia or the Internet to discover the number of bones in each part of the skeleton:

- Arm and hand
- Ribcage
- Spine
- Leg and foot
- Skull

Construct a Skeleton

Construct a skeleton from 'bits and pieces' of craft items.

For example you could use pipe cleaners, cord, a string of pearls/beads or cotton reels.

Can you think of anything else that might be useful?

Brilliant Publications   Thinking Strategies for the Successful Classroom, 5–7 Year Olds

Renzulli's Enrichment Triad

by **Rosalind Curtis**

Overview for the Classroom Teacher

RENZULLI'S TRIAD NOTES

Introduction to Renzulli's Enrichment Triad Model

The Enrichment Triad Model was devised by Joseph Renzulli in 1983 as a framework to provide pupils with the skills to carry out their own research investigations. Renzulli believes that all pupils should be given the opportunity to develop higher-order thinking skills and pursue enriched high-end learning.

When implementing the Enrichment Triad Model in the classroom, the teacher's priority is the development of independence and encouragement of self-directed learning. The open-endedness of this model gives pupils the freedom to make choices about topics, resources and manner of presentation. Teachers will also find a freedom in structure that allows them to guide their pupils through investigations and projects step by step, while still being able to change the process to suit the needs of individual pupils.

The Three Types of Activities

There are three types of activities within the Triad Model. They are:

Type I – exploratory experiences. Pupils' interests are identified. Pupils are given the opportunity to explore something new and extend their learning within a familiar topic.

Type II – group training activities. These activities promote the development of thinking and feeling processes with a major focus on advanced levels of thinking. These activities provide pupils with the necessary skills to carry out individual and small-group investigations and include:

- Creative and critical thinking skills
- Decision making
- Problem solving
- Communication skills
- Research skills

These activities develop 'learning how to learn' skills. They focus on:

- Becoming more creative
- Research techniques, and
- How to use different types of equipment.

Type III – individual and/or small-group investigations of real issues. Pupils use appropriate methods of research and inquiry and develop management plans to aid in completion of the investigation.

Type I and II enrichment activities provide the basic skills needed for pupils to carry out their own or group investigations. Type III enrichment activities require a high level of commitment from the pupils and actively engage them in the learning process by expecting them to add new knowledge, ideas or products to a field of study. (**Note:** ensure that pupils have participated in Type I and Type II activities before embarking on a Type III activity.)

All three types of enrichment activities are interrelated to a high degree within the model. The diagram below illustrates this interrelation.

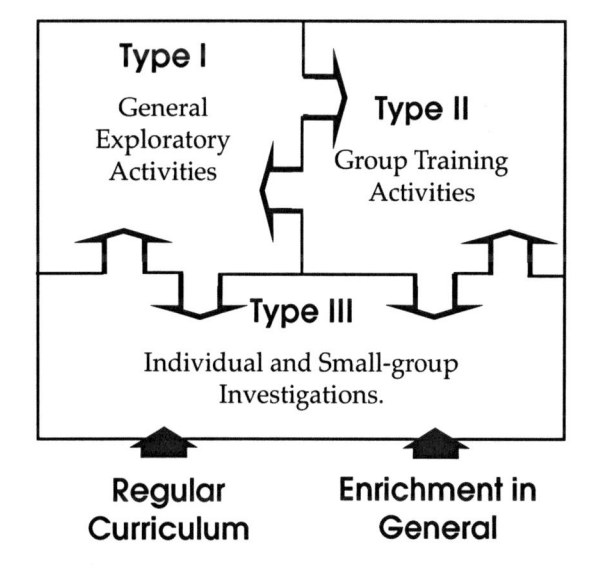

Type I – General Exploratory Activities

Type II – Group Training Activities

Type III – Individual and Small-group Investigations.

Regular Curriculum | Enrichment in General

RENZULLI'S TRIAD NOTES

Overview for the Classroom Teacher

Classroom Management

The Enrichment Triad Model emphasizes high-quality outcomes for pupils that reflect the amount of understanding and the depth of thought of participating pupils. Depending upon ability in relation to the task at hand, pupils may start at any point within the model. However, allowing pupils to embark on Type III activities without background knowledge and training (Type I and II activities) may result in a poor or less-than-worthwhile investigation.

Type I

Pupils need to be given freedom to explore a variety of topics. This exploration must be purposeful and pupils must come up with some ideas for what they would like to study and how they will go about this.

For example: A pupil may be interested in insects. The pupil then looks at material related to insects and develops questions to be investigated. These may include:

◆ Why do insects have only six legs?

◆ Do all insects have the same body structure?

◆ What does an insect do?

The pupil will also come up with a plan to find the information to answer these questions. For example:

◆ An attendant at a local museum

◆ Finding and observing insects in their natural habitat

Teachers need to help pupils identify areas of study and stimulate interest. To start the process, ask pupils to talk about their interests. Once a pupil has identified an area of interest, the teacher needs to keep checking on progress by holding formal and informal meetings to discuss findings.

Type I activities should assist the teacher in deciding which Type II activities need to be taught to particular groups of pupils.

Type II

As these activities are training exercises to help the pupil deal more effectively with finding content, the teacher must ensure that the skills are first taught in a content-free lesson. Once the skills are internalized the pupil can apply them to a specific task.

These skills focus on critical analysis, problem solving and divergent and creative thinking.

Type III

Not all pupils pursue an individual or small-group investigation for every topic. Type III enrichment activities are designed to:

◆ Foster a desire to find out more about a topic of interest

◆ Provide an opportunity for those pupils who have shown interest, willingness and commitment to carry out an investigation of their own

◆ Actively engage pupils in the formulation of a real issue and decision on a plan of action

◆ Encourage pupils to produce new information for their topic and to present their findings to audiences for whom there is some relevance

Renzulli's Enrichment Triad in Literacy

General

- Create learning/interest centres that cater for diverse interests and learning styles (see page 8).
- Involve mentors or peer tutors.
- Encourage pupils to participate fully in Type II activities.
- Ensure that pupils' communication skills (speaking, writing, listening and reading) are developed efficiently through activities that are exciting and relevant.

Type I

- Hold a class brainstorming session to identify an area of interest or theme. Compile a list of these and vote for the most popular. Ask pupils to think of information they wish to pursue in the chosen theme.
- Invite guest speakers to talk to pupils about different topics related to theme work.
- Create learning/interest centres related to the theme under study (see page 8). Include items to provoke curiosity rather than simply present information. Encourage pupils to create these centres themselves. More than one learning interest centre can be created simultaneously.
- Divide the class into the number of learning/interest centres and, over a number of days, allow pupils to explore each one.
- Trips to relevant venues are ideal for this exploratory phase. If possible, link the trip to one of the popular learning interest centres.

Type II

- Devise simple research projects to develop the research skills of finding, recording and reporting information. For example:
  - Volume research: 'Find out all you can about one of the planets in our solar system.'
  - Focused research: 'Choose a famous person and find out why that person is famous.'
  - Explanatory research: 'Find out why dinosaurs are no longer on Earth.'

- Ask pupils to devise questions for surveys that will involve gathering and interpreting information. For example:
  - 'How many of our class have red cars?'
  - 'How do we get to school?'
- Ask pupils to think creatively about solutions to different problems. For example:
  - 'What can we do with all of the hair that people have cut each year?'
  - 'How could we recycle daily rubbish?'
- Help pupils to develop questioning skills. Some useful exercises for this include:
  - Having read a story to the class, ask pupils to write two questions about each character, if they can.
  - Show pupils an unfamiliar object and ask them to think of some questions that will help them establish what the object is.
  - Give pupils the answers to a list of questions and ask them to suggest the questions that have given rise to these. For example: A: I do not like brussels sprouts./Q: What is your least favourite vegetable? What is your least favourite food? What vegetables don't you like?

Type III

- Help pupils to develop their investigation plan consisting of three parts:
  - Aim: what they want to find out.
  - Method: how they are going to find it out.
  - Report: how they will present their findings (to the teacher or class).
- Set aside regular times when pupils can meet with their mentor to discuss progress.
- Organize a forum time when pupils can present their investigations to their peers or invited guests.

RENZULLI'S TRIAD — Literacy Worksheet 23

Name:

Management Strategies:

Type I – Interest Identification

1 Draw four things you would like to find out more about.

[IDEAS | IDEAS]
[IDEAS | Ideas]
[| IDEAS]

2 Find another pupil who has one drawing the same as you.

That person's name is _____ .

3 With this person, write some questions that will help you find out more about the thing you are interested in.

Q1 _____

Q2 _____

Q3 _____

4 Find another two people who are interested in the same thing as you and your friend.

These two people are _____ and _____ .

5 In your group of four, think of some ways that you could find the answers to your questions above.

Thinking Strategies for the Successful Classroom, 5–7 Year Olds

Brilliant Publications

© Blake Education Pty Ltd. 2004

Name:

Management Strategies:
★ ■ ▼

RENZULLI'S TRIAD
Literacy
Worksheet 24

Type II – Creative Thinking Skills, Originality

1 Draw a picture of an aeroplane that you could make out of paper.

2 Make this aeroplane and fly it.

3 Draw what happened when you flew your aeroplane.

4 What could you do to make your aeroplane better?

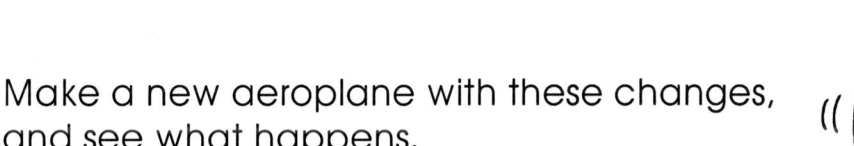

I could _____
_____
_____
_____
_____

5 Make a new aeroplane with these changes, and see what happens.

6 Draw what happened.

7 What else could you do to make your aeroplane fly further and higher?

I could _____
_____
_____
_____
_____

8 Find some friends and fly your aeroplanes in a contest to see whose is the best.

Brilliant Publications — Thinking Strategies for the Successful Classroom, 5–7 Year Olds — 73

Renzulli's Enrichment Triad in Maths

General

- For more able pupils, use individual contracts and guidelines for the completion of work.
- Collect hands-on resources so that pupils can explore concepts while manipulating material in real-life situations.
- Involve pupils in games that require the application of problem-solving skills such as dominoes, Uno, noughts and crosses and Chinese Chequers.
- Use 'skill centres' (see 'learning/interest centres') that help pupils apply and extend particular skills (numeration, patterning, problem solving, money) in real-life situations.

Type I

- Create opportunities for pupils to explore properties of numbers using hands-on materials. For example:

    Arranging 15 counters in as many different ways as they can using addition, multiplication and place value, and writing the corresponding number sentences.

- Ask pupils to match mathematical terms with cards that show that term being applied. For example:

addition	15 + 7
time	7:30pm
shape	triangle

- Ask pupils to brainstorm all the things they do during the day that involve maths.

Type II

- Conduct surveys in which pupils collect, record and interpret data. For example:
    - A whole-class interview about which pets they have at home.

    Follow up with evaluative questions:
    - 'What is the third most popular pet?'
    - 'If you owned a pet shop, which four animals would sell best?'

- Create opportunities for pupils to make and check predictions. For example:
    - 'Which object will weigh more?'
    - 'Which object is longer/shorter?'
    - 'Which group of counters has more in it?'
    - 'Which bundle of blocks is even?'

- Provide problems for pupils to solve. For example:
    - 'A farmer has 12 sheep and 15 cows. How many animals does the farmer have altogether?'
    - 'If a school has 12 classes and there are 25 pupils in each class, how many pupils are there altogether?'
    - 'How many different ways can you express the number 285?'

- Encourage pupils to complete small research projects. For example:
    - 'How have numbers been written down in the past?'
    - 'What ways do we measure time?'
    - 'When would a butcher use maths?'

Type III

- Ask pupils to write a plan of action prior to starting their investigation.
- Ask pupils how they will present their findings and who their audience will be.
- Ask pupils to explain how they carried out their investigation and the methods they used.

Name:

Management Strategies:

RENZULLI'S TRIAD
Maths
Worksheet 25

Type II – Research
Sundials

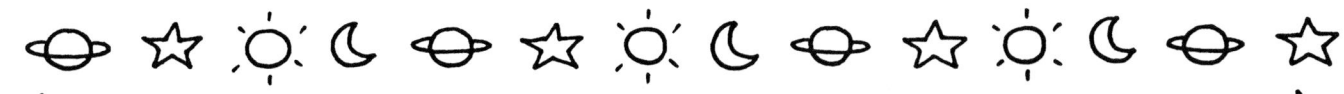

1. Draw some instruments that have been used to measure time.

2. Draw a sundial below and describe what it will be made from.

   My sundial will look like this: My sundial is made from:

   _____
   _____
   _____
   _____
   _____

3. Explain how sundials work.

   _____
   _____
   _____

4. Where would be the best place to put your sundial in the playground? _____

5. On the back of this sheet, illustrate what your sundial will look like in the playground.

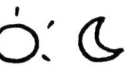

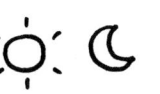

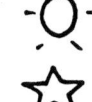

Brilliant Publications — Thinking Strategies for the Successful Classroom, 5–7 Year Olds

Name:

Management Strategies:

Type II – Group Research
Television Habits

People in our group are:

_____

Conduct a survey to find out:

| How many hours of TV do your friends watch each day? | What is their favourite programme? | Which programme they do not like to watch? |

Questions our group will ask are:

1 _____   2 _____

3 _____   4 _____

On the back of this sheet, draw up a table to record the answers.

Show your results as a:

Picture graph	Bar graph	Your choice

76   Thinking Strategies for the Successful Classroom, 5–7 Year Olds   Brilliant Publications

Renzulli's Enrichment Triad in Science

General

- Create learning/interest centres (see page 8) related to themes across curriculum areas that reflect the interests of the pupils. For example: dinosaurs, ecology, looking at insects and bugs and astronomy (with a focus on the planets and stars).

- Encourage pupils to question what they see in terms of 'How … ?' or 'Why did that happen?'

- Encourage pupils' natural curiosity by presentations that show an end result (rather than simply giving information about the topic). For example, construct a volcano that actually explodes.

- Help pupils to look at a problem from many different angles and come up with more than one solution.

Type I

- Visit the local science centre where pupils can have hands-on experience in all facets of science.

- Allow pupils to carry out simple experiments under adult supervision.

- Hold an 'animal day' where pupils bring in pets and visitors bring in unusual animals such as snakes, parrots or llamas.

- Make available pictures and books on a variety of different topics related to a theme or pupils' interests.

Type II

- Promote discussion among pupils of solutions to problems. For example:
  - 'How could Jack and Jill have taken the water down the hill without carrying a heavy bucket?'
  - 'What would we do if there were no telephones?'
  - 'How could we help people get better if antibiotics had not been invented?'

- Ask pupils to chart the weather over a period of time. Encourage them to make some assumptions about the weather and the season. For example: 'It is getting colder because it is now winter.'

- Ask pupils to complete small-scale investigations. Let them discuss ways to investigate these questions and how they will present their findings. For example:
  - 'What type of food do we eat during the day?'
  - 'Is it good for us or not?'

- Allow pupils to complete research projects that will help them identify ways to gather information and record and summarize data. For example:
  - 'What does the moon look like?'
  - 'How do fish swim?'
  - 'How do plants grow?'

Type III

- Ask pupils to plan how their investigation will take place and the methods they will use to support their hypothesis or meet the goals they have identified.

- Ask pupils what the relevance of their investigation is to them personally.

- Hold a 'Science Fair' so that pupils can present their findings to a variety of people.

Name:

Type II – Small-scale Investigation
Food Diary

1 Keep a diary for one week of what you eat at school.

Monday	Tuesday	Wednesday	Thursday	Friday
Break Time	Break Time	Break Time	Break Time	Break Time
Lunch	Lunch	Lunch	Lunch	Lunch

2 Sort these into the five food groups below.

Fats & sugars	Cereals & Bread	Meat & Fish	Dairy	Fruit & Vegetables

3 Which group has the most food in it?

_____

4 Compare your diary and chart with those belonging to some other members of your class.

5 On a separate piece of paper, make a graph to show how much from each food group is eaten by you and your friends in one week. Write three statements about the information in your graph.

Name:

Management Strategies:

RENZULLI'S TRIAD
Science
Worksheet 28

Type I – Predictions and Checking
Visit to the Supermarket

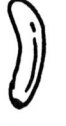

Before you go:

1. On the back of this sheet, draw four different jobs you think you'll see being done at the supermarket.

2. Write down some food items you think you'll see in these food sections.

Dairy Section	Meat Section	Bakery	Fruit & Veg.	Frozen Foods

When you have visited the supermarket:

3. Draw four jobs that you saw people doing at the supermarket.

4. Write down some food items you actually found in these food sections.

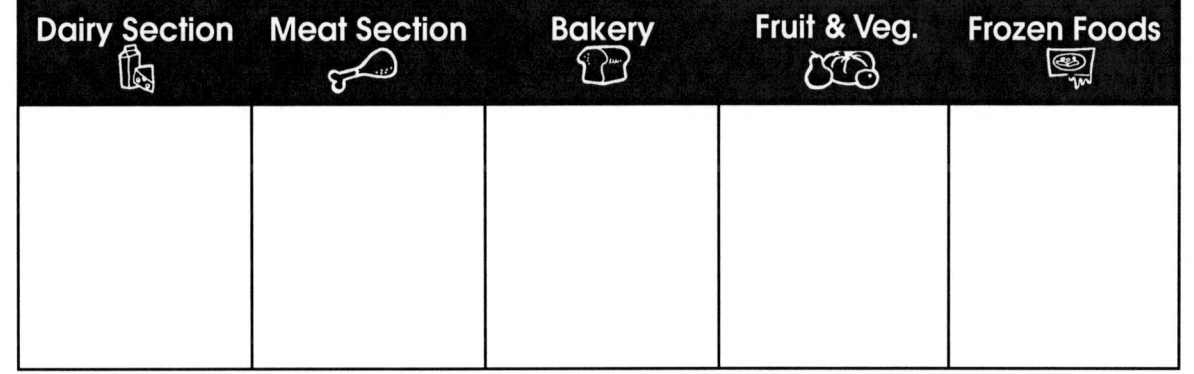

Dairy Section	Meat Section	Bakery	Fruit & Veg.	Frozen Foods

5. Did your predictions match with what you actually saw happening at the supermarket? _____

_____

Brilliant Publications		Thinking Strategies for the Successful Classroom, 5–7 Year Olds

Gardner's Multiple Intelligences

by **Fay Holbert** and **Margaret Bishop**

Overview for the Classroom Teacher

GARDNER'S MULTIPLE INTELLIGENCES

NOTES

Introduction to Howard Gardner's 'Multiple Intelligences' Theory

Gardner defines intelligence as 'the ability to solve problems or to create products that are valued within one or more cultural setting/s'. He maintains that it should be possible to identify an individual's educational profile at an early age, and then draw upon this knowledge to enhance that person's educational opportunities and options. An educator should be able to channel individuals with unusual talents into special enrichment activities. To this end, he has developed a framework, building on the theory of multiple intelligences, that can be applied to any educational situation.

Because of Gardner's work, many educators believe that education is not merely a means of selecting a few children and making them leaders, but a way of developing the latent talents of the entire population in diverse ways.

If we are to understand our children's potential, we must take into consideration all of their abilities and not just those that can be tested with standardized instruments such as an IQ test. What is important in educational terms is not which intelligences we are strongest in, but our own particular blend of strengths and weaknesses.

The importance attached to the IQ however is not entirely inappropriate – the score does predict a person's ability to achieve in school subjects. Its limitation is that it predicts little of the successes in later life.

So, what of the wider range of performances that are valued in different parts of the world? For example: a 12-year-old boy from the Caroline Islands who has shown some ability is selected by his elders to learn how to become a master sailor and undertake a study of navigation, geography and the stars, and a 15-year-old Iranian youth who has committed to heart the entire Koran and mastered the Arabic language will train to be a teacher and religious leader.

It is obvious that these two young people are displaying intelligent behaviour, and it is equally clear that the present method of assessing intellect is not going to allow an accurate assessment of their potential or their achievements. Only if we expand and rethink our views of what counts as human intellect will we, as educators, be able to devise more appropriate ways of assessing it, and more effective ways of educating it.

Gardner's 'Intelligence's Are:

- Verbal/Linguistic
- Logical/Mathematical
- Visual/Spatial
- Bodily/Kinaesthetic
- Musical/Rhythmical
- Interpersonal
- Intrapersonal

Recently Gardner has added a new intelligence: Nature/Environmental.

Learning/Interest Centres

The classroom teacher should give equal time and attention to each intelligence every day. One way to achieve this is to maintain various learning/interest centres in the classroom (see page 8). For example:

- The William Shakespeare Centre **(Verbal/Linguistic)**
- The Albert Einstein Centre **(Logical/Mathematical)**
- The Leonardo da Vinci Centre **(Visual/Spatial)**
- The Roger Bannister Centre **(Bodily/Kinaesthetic)**
- The Wolfgang Amadeus Mozart Centre **(Musical/Rhythmical)**
- The Mary Seacole Centre **(Interpersonal)**
- The Helen Keller Centre **(Intrapersonal)**
- The David Attenborough Centre **(Nature/Environmental)**

A Note About This Section

This section looks at two themes from the perspective of the various 'intelligences'.

GARDNER'S MULTIPLE INTELLIGENCES NOTES

Overview for the Classroom Teacher

Details and Description of Gardner's 'Multiple Intelligences'

Verbal/Linguistic (V/L)

The pupil who enjoys words – reading, writing, storytelling and humour/jokes. He/she participates eagerly in debates, story/poetry writing and journal/diary keeping and has a sensitivity to language.
- *Writer, poet, novelist, journalist, psycho-linguist (L/M), signing.*

Logical/Mathematical (L/M)

The pupil who loves numbers, patterns, relationships and formulae. He/she shines at mathematics, reasoning, logic, problem solving and deciphering codes and enjoys pattern games, calculation, number sequences and outlining.
- *Scientist, mathematician, engineer, technician.*

Visual/Spatial (V/S)

The pupil who loves drawing, building, designing, creating, visualizing colours and pictures and observing and creating patterns/designs. He/she enjoys creating models, mind mapping and pretending and has an active imagination.
- *Artist, cartographer, navigator, decorator, chess player.*

Bodily/Kinaesthetic (B/K)

The pupil who has to touch, move and handle objects. He/she enjoys dance, drama, role-play, mime, sports games, physical gestures, martial arts and is great with body control, refining movement, expression through movement, inventing, interaction.
- *Athlete, surgeon (L/M), dancer/choreographer (M/R).*

Musical/Rhythmical (M/R)

The pupil who loves sounds, melody, rhythm, playing instruments, singing and vocal sounds/tones. He/she needs to be involved with music composition/creation and music performances and enjoys percussion, humming, environmental/instrumental sounds and tonal and rhythmic patterns.
- *Musician, composer, sound engineer (L/M), music critic (V/L).*

Interpersonal (Ier)

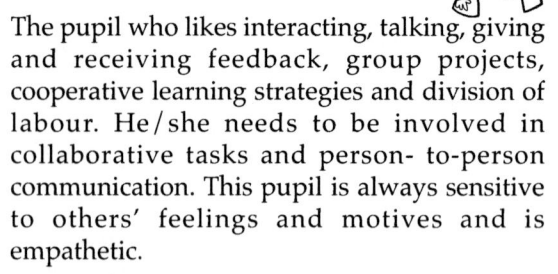

The pupil who likes interacting, talking, giving and receiving feedback, group projects, cooperative learning strategies and division of labour. He/she needs to be involved in collaborative tasks and person- to-person communication. This pupil is always sensitive to others' feelings and motives and is empathetic.
- *Administrator, coach, mental health, physician (L/M), teacher (various).*

Intrapersonal (Ira)

The pupil who wants to work alone and pursue personal interests, understands self and has introspective feelings and dreams. He/she displays silent reflective methods, higher-order reasoning and metacognition techniques, emotional processing, focus/concentration skills, complex guided imagery and 'centring' practices.
- *Writer (V/L), inventor (L/M).*

Nature/Environmental (N/E)

Recently, Gardner has included an eighth intelligence which he calls 'Nature/Environmental'. Not a lot of information is yet available from Gardner on this 'intelligence', but it is summarized as one involving the recognition and classification of species in the environment, and how we can best preserve this environment for the greatest benefit to all.
- *Veterinarian, zoologist, botanist, national park ranger, landscape gardener (V/L), florist.*

Note: the children illustrated here appear on the task cards and worksheets that follow to indicate the 'intelligence' to which that activity is primarily targeted.

Gardner's Multiple Intelligences, Activities

Theme: Land Transport

Many of the activities that follow are not exclusive to one intelligence, but may involve two or more. For example, those asking for illustrations involve Visual/Spatial and those requiring oral and/or written presentations involve Verbal/Linguistic etc.

Where questions could be answered with a 'yes' or 'no' response, probe further.

Verbal/Linguistic

- What do we mean by 'transport'? Build up a vocabulary for land 'transport' – pre- wheel to modern day.
- Which animals might have been used to assist with transport?
- What forms of transport do you use? Compare your responses with those of your friends.

Logical/Mathematical

- Time how long it takes to walk to school.
- How does this time compare with cycling or being driven to school? Explain.
- Is your time the same as/similar to your friends' times? Explain.
- How far do you live from the school/ shopping centre?

Visual/Spatial

- Do cars look the same now as they did 10, 20 or 50 years ago? How are they different/ the same?
- Has the way people travel changed much over the last 100, 200 or 500 years? How?
- Design a type of land transport that would be suitable for young people to use to go to school or do the family shopping.

Bodily/Kinaesthetic

- Which sports involve using types of transport? What types?
- What is the same about all the contests that involve types of transport? Explain.
- How could you improve the vehicles used?
- Why are there different types of transport?

Musical/Rhythmical

- What 'travelling songs' do you know?
- Ask the class to guess how you are travelling when you:
  - Mime different rhythms of transport.
  - Create sounds of travelling/transport.

Interpersonal

- How is transport useful?
- How is transport a danger?
- What are we doing to try to make transport less dangerous?
- Why don't these ideas always work?

Intrapersonal

- If you had to travel a short distance (a kilometre or less), how would you travel?
- If you had to travel a long way (thousands of kilometres), how would you travel?
- If you could travel anywhere at all: where would you go; when would you go; how long would you stay; and how would you get there?
- If you lived 100 years ago, how would you have preferred to travel about?
- What type of transport would you like to own now? Why?

Nature/Environmental

- If you couldn't ask anyone, and you wanted to find out about transport in the local community, how would you go about it? You want to know: if there is transport, what type there is and where to find it.
- Does transport damage the environment? How?
- How could this be reduced or prevented?

GARDNER'S MULTIPLE INTELLIGENCES TASK CARDS

Activities for Land Transport

Differences

Can you think of other children who would use different types of transport from the kind you use?

Why are their needs different from yours?

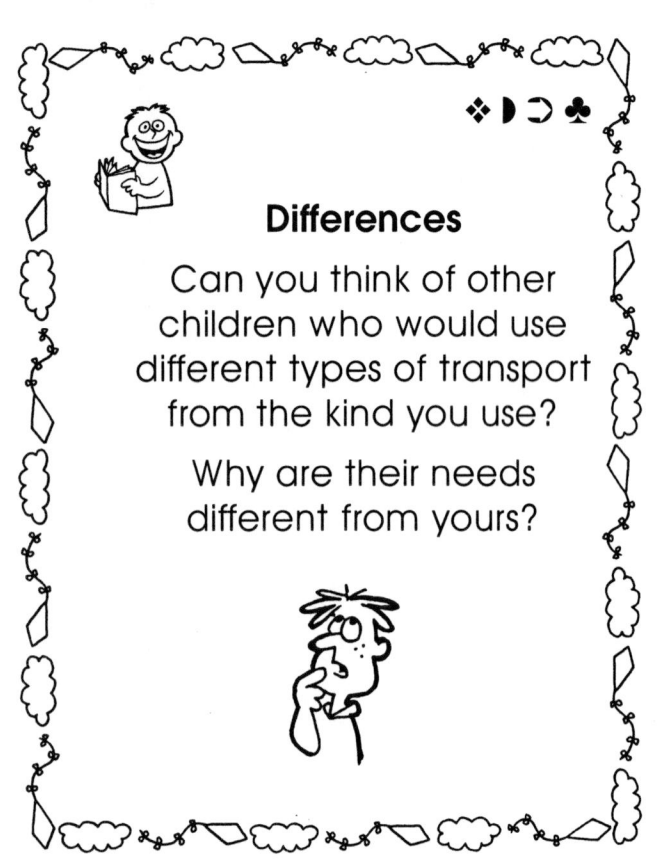

Cycle Safety

Make a list of the safety equipment that all bicycles and cyclists should have.

How Much Is It?

Think about how much it costs:
- to walk to school
- to cycle to school
- to come by car

Make a list of these costs and compare the methods.

Which costs the least?

Getting to School

Survey your class about the types of transport they use on their way to school.

Who:
- walks
- cycles
- is driven
- catches the bus
- uses other methods?

Activities for Land Transport

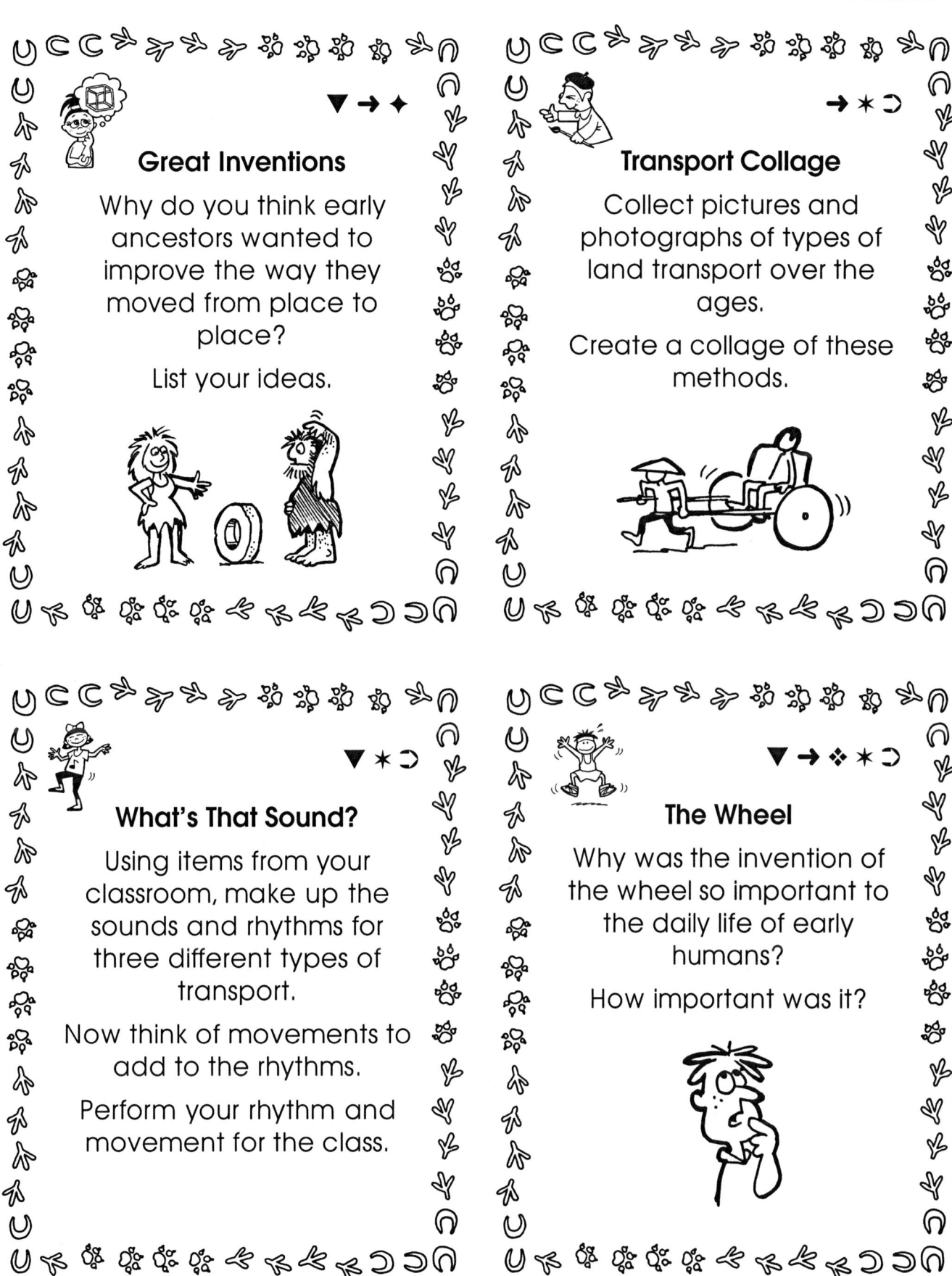

GARDNER'S MULTIPLE INTELLIGENCES TASK CARDS

Great Inventions

Why do you think early ancestors wanted to improve the way they moved from place to place?

List your ideas.

Transport Collage

Collect pictures and photographs of types of land transport over the ages.

Create a collage of these methods.

What's That Sound?

Using items from your classroom, make up the sounds and rhythms for three different types of transport.

Now think of movements to add to the rhythms.

Perform your rhythm and movement for the class.

The Wheel

Why was the invention of the wheel so important to the daily life of early humans?

How important was it?

Activities for Land Transport

Comparisons

What are the advantages and disadvantages of these types of transport?

Walking	Going by coach	Horse riding
Driving a tractor	Cycling	Using a skateboard
Catching a bus	Taking a tram	Skiing
Riding a motorbike		

Remote Transport

Imagine that you live in these places:

The Desert, Antarctica, The Jungle, The Alps

Draw pictures of how you would travel about there. There may be more than one way to travel in some areas.

Moving Goods

Transport is not just used to move people around. It is also used to move goods from place to place.

List the good things and bad things about these ways of carrying goods:

Lorry, Car and trailer, Train

Activities for Land Transport

GARDNER'S MULTIPLE INTELLIGENCES TASK CARDS

Olden Days

Ask your grandparents or elderly friends about the land transport they used when they were your age.

Ask someone from another country about the transport there.

Draw pictures of the types of transport you find out about.

Animals & Transport

Make a list of the animals that were used in the past to transport things.

Which animals are still used in this way?

Collect pictures and photographs of these animals at work.

Special Vehicles

Have you ever seen types of transport that have been changed to help people who have a disability?

Explain to your class:
- What you have seen
- How it would help

GARDNER'S MULTIPLE INTELLIGENCES Worksheet 29

Name:

Management Strategies:

Environment Watch

1. What kind of damage has been done to the environment by modern methods of transport?

   Make a list here: _____
   _____
   _____

2. Draw a picture of some of the damage that has been caused by the various types of transport.

3. Can anything be done to improve this, or is it too late?

   Write your thoughts here: _____
   _____
   _____

88 Thinking Strategies for the Successful Classroom, 5–7 Year Olds Brilliant Publications

© Blake Education Pty Ltd. 2004. This page may be photocopied for use by the purchasing institution only.

Name:

Management Strategies:
❖ ✖ ▲

GARDNER'S MULTIPLE INTELLIGENCES
Worksheet 30

My Favourite Transport

1. If you were old enough, what type of transport would you like to be in charge of?

   I would like to be in charge of: _____

   _____

2. Why would you like this?

   I would like this because: _____

   _____

3. What would you do in it?

   I would: _____

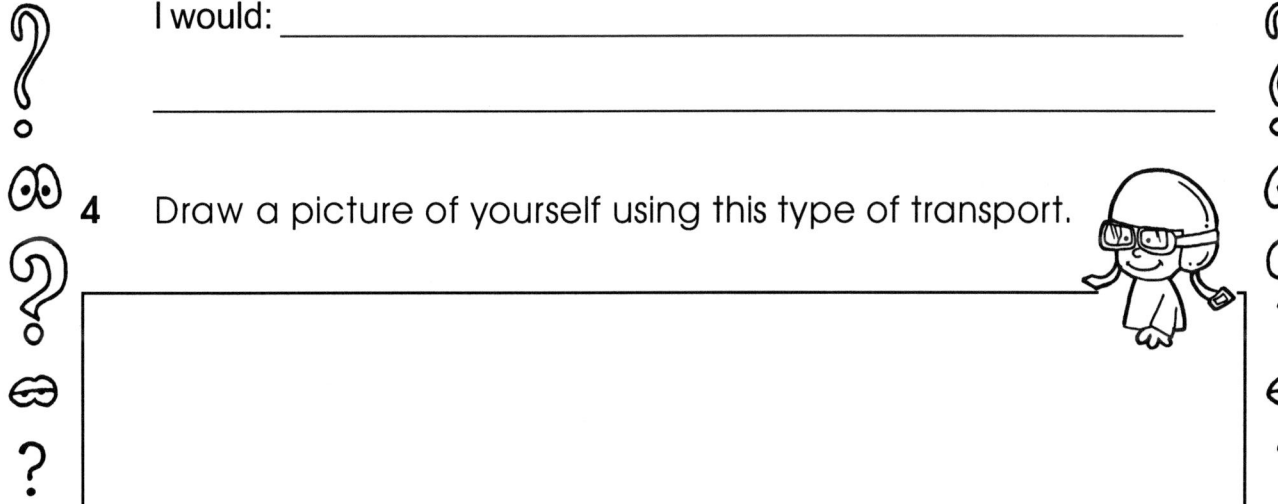

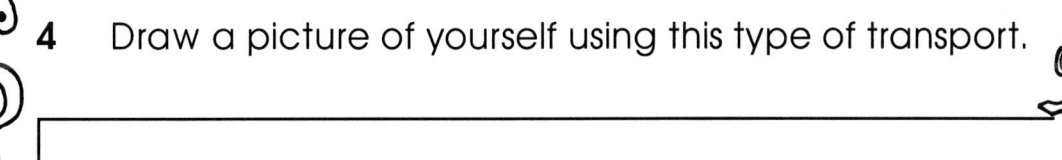

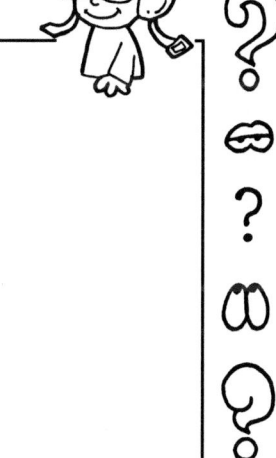

   _____

4. Draw a picture of yourself using this type of transport.

Brilliant Publications　　Thinking Strategies for the Successful Classroom, 5–7 Year Olds　　89

GARDNER'S MULTIPLE INTELLIGENCES Worksheet 31

Name:

Management Strategies:

Bicycles and Things

1. The first bicycle was built in England over 350 years ago. It had no pedals. Riders had to push it along with their feet! Draw this invention.

   Bicycle from the year 1642

2. Now think about a 21st-century 'personal transport machine'.

   How would it move? _____

   What would it be made of? _____

   What would it look like? _____

   Draw your invention here.

   Personal Transport Machine for the Year 2042

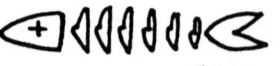

90   Thinking Strategies for the Successful Classroom, 5–7 Year Olds   Brilliant Publications

Gardner's Multiple Intelligences, Activities

Theme: Food

Many of the suggested activities involve more than one of the intelligences. Pupils should be encouraged to attempt a wide range of activities and to be aware of the various intelligences they are using.

Verbal/Linguistic (V/L)

- What is 'food'? What criteria can we use to decide if something is 'food' or not?
- Who or what needs food? Make a list of all animals (including humans) and plants that need food.
- Where would you find food? List all the places in your home, school, community, city and beyond.

Logical/Mathematical (L/M)

- Make a graph of all the different foods that everyone in the class has brought for lunch.
- What are the five most popular foods to include in school lunches?
- Conduct a survey of what food is sold in your school canteen.

Visual/Spatial (V/S)

- Cut pictures of food from magazines and supermarket catalogues and make a food collage.
- Has food been the subject of paintings or drawings of artists? Find examples and compare them. Are some more realistic than others?
- Design a cover for a cookery book that includes your favourite food.

Bodily/Kinaesthetic (B/K)

- What foods help us grow healthy bodies?
- What sporting events or games have food items as part of the equipment? For example egg and spoon race or apple bobbing.
- Does anyone in the class have any food allergies? What are the symptoms?
- Conduct a 'blind' taste and touch test of common foods.

Musical/Rhythmical (M/R)

- What 'food' songs do you know?
- Make up a jingle or rap to encourage people to eat healthy food.
- What songs are used on television or in radio advertisements about foods?

Interpersonal (Ier)

- What community events or family gatherings have food as a focus?
- What special types of food are used for different celebrations?
- What food from other cultures have you eaten?

Intrapersonal (Ira)

- What are your favourite or least favourite foods? Compare your responses with those of your friends.
- Design your favourite three-course meal.
- Share a funny or unusual experience you have had involving food.

Nature/Environmental (N/E)

- Trace the origin of food in your lunch box, eg wheat farm, fruit orchard etc.
- Conduct a survey of the packaging in school lunches. Is any of it recyclable?
- If you were lost in the jungle, how would you find food?

Activities for Food – Seafood

GARDNER'S MULTIPLE INTELLIGENCES TASK CARDS

Food from the Sea

Draw pictures to show all the foods we gather from the sea.

Describe how the different types of seafood are caught.

Farming Seafood

Some seafood is now farmed. What are some of the good things and some of the bad things about farming fish and other seafood?

How would sea farming be different from land farming?

Seafood

Different cultures prepare and eat different types of seafood.

Make a list of all the different seafood that can be eaten. Collect recipes from different cultures.

Saving Dolphins and Whales

Dolphins, whales, sea turtles and sharks are often caught in the huge nets used in commercial fishing. Design a new way of catching fish that would not endanger other sea creatures.

92   Thinking Strategies for the Successful Classroom, 5–7 Year Olds   Brilliant Publications

© Blake Education Pty Ltd 2004

This page may be photocopied for use by the purchasing institution only.

Activities for Food – Celebrations

GARDNER'S MULTIPLE INTELLIGENCES TASK CARDS

Birthday Food

Plan a menu for your next birthday.

Draw pictures of all the special food you will have at your party.

Make a shopping list for your party.

Easter Food

Why are chocolate and sugar eggs and rabbits given as gifts at Easter?

Do other cultures have the same or different customs?

Christmas Food

Christmas is a time for families and friends to give gifts and to share special meals.

What special food is prepared at Christmas?

Shiny new 'sixpences' used to be hidden in the Christmas pudding as a surprise for the eaters. Why do you think this was done?

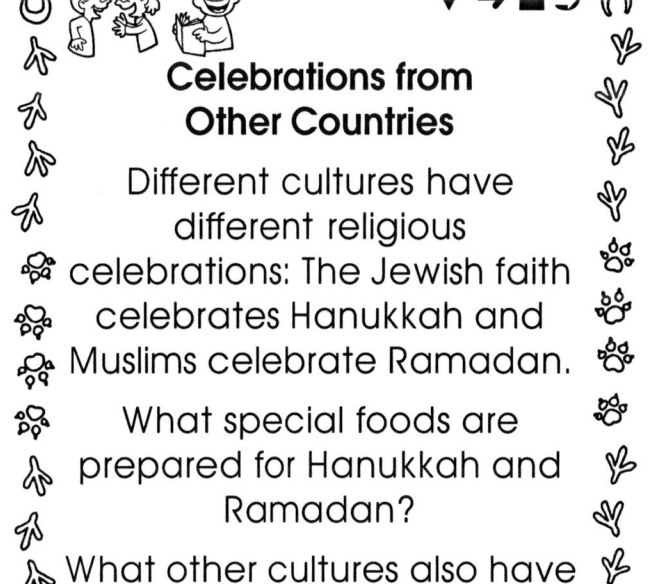

Celebrations from Other Countries

Different cultures have different religious celebrations: The Jewish faith celebrates Hanukkah and Muslims celebrate Ramadan.

What special foods are prepared for Hanukkah and Ramadan?

What other cultures also have celebrations where food is specially prepared?

Activities for Food – Past and Future

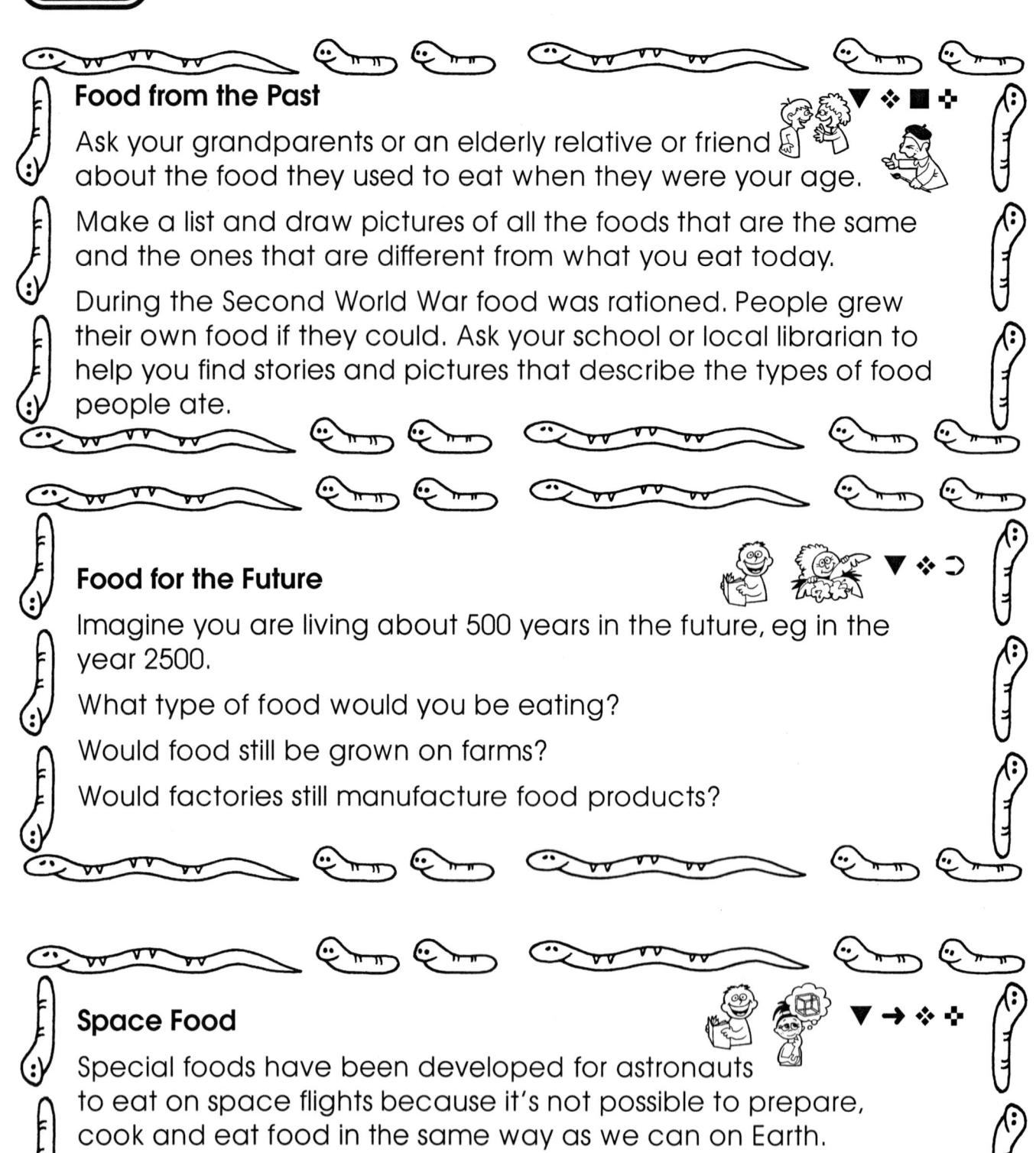

Food from the Past

Ask your grandparents or an elderly relative or friend about the food they used to eat when they were your age.

Make a list and draw pictures of all the foods that are the same and the ones that are different from what you eat today.

During the Second World War food was rationed. People grew their own food if they could. Ask your school or local librarian to help you find stories and pictures that describe the types of food people ate.

Food for the Future

Imagine you are living about 500 years in the future, eg in the year 2500.

What type of food would you be eating?

Would food still be grown on farms?

Would factories still manufacture food products?

Space Food

Special foods have been developed for astronauts to eat on space flights because it's not possible to prepare, cook and eat food in the same way as we can on Earth.

If you were planning a menu to take on a space flight, what foods would you include?

How would you make sure that the food for the astronauts was healthy and tasty?

Name: _____

Management Strategies: ▼ → ◆ ◆ ♣

GARDNER'S MULTIPLE INTELLIGENCES
Worksheet 32

Japanese Food

1 Find out what foods people like eating in Japan.
   Make a list here: _____
   _____
   _____

2 Draw a picture of some of the food people eat in Japan.

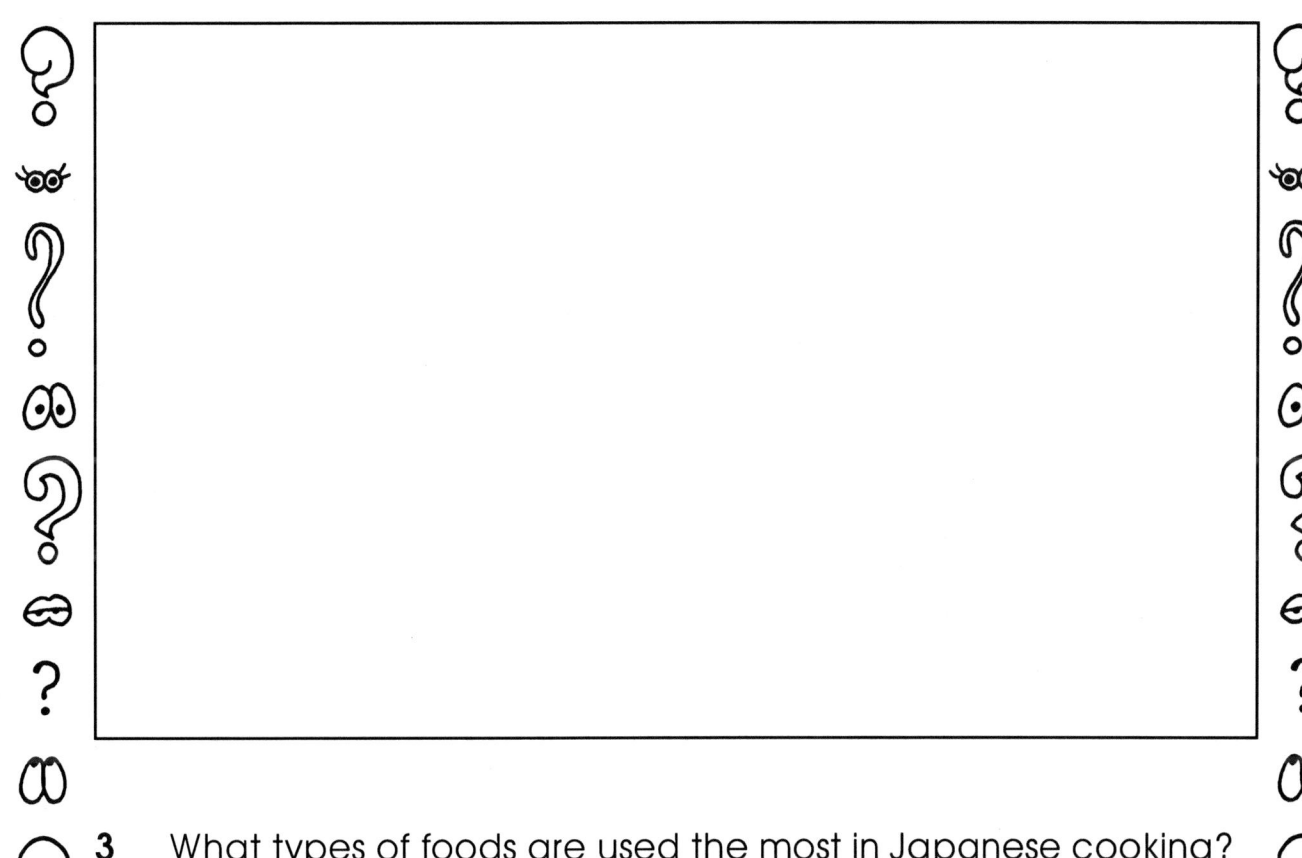

[   ]

3 What types of foods are used the most in Japanese cooking?
   Write your answers here: _____
   _____
   _____

Brilliant Publications   Thinking Strategies for the Successful Classroom, 5–7 Year Olds

GARDNER'S MULTIPLE INTELLIGENCES — Worksheet 33

Name:

Management Strategies:

My Favourite Food

1 List your 10 favourite foods.

My favourite foods are:

1 _____ 2 _____ 3 _____
4 _____ 5 _____ 6 _____
7 _____ 8 _____ 9 _____
10 _____

2 Why are these your favourite foods?

_____
_____

3 Invent a 'mystery' recipe that could be sold in a restaurant or fast-food cafe. Think of an interesting name for your recipe.

My 'Mystery' Recipe is: _____

_____

4 Design a poster to advertise your mystery recipe.

Thinking Strategies for the Successful Classroom, 5–7 Year Olds — Brilliant Publications

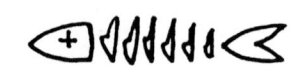

Carterhatch Infant School
Carterhatch Lane
Enfield
EN1 4JY
Tel. 0208 804 6886
Fax 0208 373 7323
www.carterhatch-inf.enfield.sch.uk

Printed in the United Kingdom
by Lightning Source UK Ltd.
126498UK00001B/131-138/A

9 781905 780037